NEW STUDIES IN MYSTICAL
RELIGION

THE MACMILLAN COMPANY
NEW YORK · BOSTON · CHICAGO · DALLAS
ATLANTA · SAN FRANCISCO

MACMILLAN & CO., LIMITED
LONDON · BOMBAY · CALCUTTA
MELBOURNE

THE MACMILLAN CO. OF CANADA, LTD.
TORONTO

New Studies in Mystical Religion

The Ely Lectures Delivered at Union
Theological Seminary, New York
1927

BY

RUFUS M. JONES

Litt. D., D.D., LL.D., D. Theol., Professor of Philosophy in
Haverford College. Author of *Studies in Mystical Religion,
Spiritual Reformers, The World Within,* etc.

New York

THE MACMILLAN COMPANY

1927

To

the beautiful memory of my friend

BARON FRIEDRICH VON HÜGEL

the foremost interpreter of mystical religion in this generation, who strikingly illustrated the meaning of radiance in religion, and who made me see more clearly than anyone else what it means to be a member of the invisible Church

CONTENTS

INTRODUCTION

THE main attack in recent years on the validity of mysticism as a religious experience is the characteristic attack of the psychologist.[1] He insists that the experience is purely subjective and consequently lacks objective reference to any reality beyond the individual who has the experience. He brackets drug-intoxications, the spells of medicine men, hypnotic states, and hysterical trances with the exalted experiences of God which have come to mystics, and then proceeds to show that they are one and all alike "such stuff as dreams are made of"—in short, purely subjective creations.

In so far as the mystical experience is taken as a "sheer," "bare" experience, sacred in its own right, uninterpreted, and unrelated to moral and spiritual effects on life and character, the criticism carries weight. It is obvious that "mere feels,"

[1] See especially Leuba's *The Psychology of Religious Mysticism* (New York & London, 1925).

"ineffable exaltations," "unspeakable heavenly uplifts," which remain uncorrelated with the total whole of life and thought, so long as they are *that* and nothing more, give no clue to objective value, or to objective reality. There is no good ground, or sound basis, however, for limiting mystical experience to any such contracted field. The same psychological method applied to any form of sense experience in the same limited way would equally deprive *it* of objective validity. There is no way of proving that our unmediated sensations of color, of sound, of odor, of taste, of roughness or smoothness or hardness, stand for objective realities precisely like our subjective experiences of them. Two of the profoundest psychologists that ever lived, Bishop George Berkeley and David Hume, to name no others, stoutly maintained that the mental *experience* of sense qualities gives no coercive evidence of an external material world which possesses those same qualities. The method of psychological diagnosis which is believed to destroy the objective validity of mystical experience would also destroy all objective validity in every field of experience.

We owe a very great debt to the psychologist for his exact descriptions, his calm analyses, his searching criticisms. He has helped to dispel superstitions and he has taught us to discriminate *facts* in that obscure region within us where confusion all too easily reigns. But there are severe limits to his field. He must learn restraint. He must be content to give us facts and not propaganda.

Psychology as an empirical science does not profess to deal, or at least ought not to profess to deal, with ultimate questions. It studies, as accurately as it can do, what occurs in the field of consciousness. It deals with mental processes, mental reactions, and mental phenomena. It supplies us with no absolute criterion of objectivity. We need not blame the psychologist that he tends to reduce religion in all its phases to a subjective basis. He is bound to a restricted field by the rigid limitations of his science. I have no personal desire to see the field of psychology unduly circumscribed. I have no fear that an increase of the knowledge of *facts* will shatter the spiritual legacies of the race. I am only emphasizing here what most psychologists have many times themselves affirmed, that psychology as a science of mental phenomena does not invade the realm of philosophical interpretation.

The psychological "reduction" is no less obvious in the field of aesthetics than in the field of religion. The modern psychologist finds no ground for objective validity in any experience of *values*. Science admits no *values*. Beauty for a psychologist is severely limited to what is *felt and enjoyed*. As soon as one begins to find ground for beauty and sublimity in the ultimate nature of the universe itself he has transcended the method and the sphere of psychology. No empirical study of mental processes can be expected to do more than supply us with subjective *facts* and the order of their arrangement. We can merely conclude from psychological studies that men in different stages of human history have *felt* so and so, have *thought* thus and thus, and have *acted* in certain specific ways. The psychology of religion can, even when it has done its best and completest, give us no sure ground for those objective realities which seem essential to the profoundly religious soul. But no more can the method of psychology, unaided, give an objective basis for the experience of sense qualities, or for beauty experience, or for music experience, or for love experience, or for moral values. The trail of subjectivity is over them all.

Questions of validity and of objective reality are problems which concern philosophy. They lie beyond the scope and method of empirical psychology. But every now and then a psychologist joins the ranks of the dogmatists and loudly asserts conclusions which do violence to the methods of the science in which he is an expert. Haeckel spoke with weight and authority so long as he confined himself to problems of biology, but he became no more than a dogmatic assertor when he promulgated his views and theories in the fields of philosophy and religion, where his ignorance was glaringly revealed by what he wrote. Many psychologists, and peculiarly some who make dogmatic assertions about the validity of religion, show a great impatience with philosophical methods and philosophical discipline, and they often reveal a lack of familiarity with the deeper ranges and the essential significance of philosophy. The scientific method is all-sufficient for their interests and thus the empirical approach is all they care for. That is, of course, an intelligent restriction to make, so long as they are content to confine themselves to that level and to that restriction. I raise my word of protest only when the empirical scientist goes out beyond the obvious limits of his field and pronounces, authoritatively, on matters which do not belong within it, and about which he has no expert knowledge that qualifies him to speak. Psychological training *alone* gives no one authoritative ground to construct with finality theories of knowledge or to settle dogmatically the problems that arise out of our experience of spiritual values.

A vast amount of intellectual labor has in recent years been bestowed upon the nature and scope of spiritual values.[2] It is a central problem of human life. Psychology is, of course, quite rightly concerned with the study of the enjoyment of beauty, the history and the social basis of moral sentiments, with the instincts and emotions that are involved in the manifestations of "love," and in the attitudes and mental processes which characterize religious experience. But psychology as such has nothing to say, and can legitimately have nothing to say, about the ultimate metaphysical ground of these values. Do they spring from a blind driving-urge in man with no correspondent reality in the world beyond man, or do they arise in us because the universe in its deeper aspects is itself a universe which furnishes a ground for spiritual values and is essentially adapted to call them forth in us and to minister to them?

The greatest philosophers of the ages, and some of those who are best qualified to speak on

[2] The following chapters of this book will present grounds for putting mystical experience among the spiritual values.

these issues in the modern world, find solid ground for the position that the central *values* of human life carry objective reference, at least as certainly as do our perceptions of external objects. In any case the person who at the present stage of this philosophical quest insists upon sheer *subjectivity* is, to say the least, premature, superficial, and dogmatic. One of the best ways to make a contribution toward a final settlement of these issues is to clarify still further the real nature of mystical experience and to link it up with the social, the ethical, and the practical aspects of life. It has been studied in the past too much as an isolated aspect, appearing only in a few rare individuals. It has been treated as a mysterious and supernatural wonder, and not as something that is bound up with normal, healthy daily life.

The mystic, as I hope to show, is not a peculiarly favored mortal who by a lucky chance has received into his life a windfall from some heavenly Bread-fruit tree, while he lay dreaming of iridescent rainbows. He is, rather, a person who has cultivated, with more strenuous care and discipline than others have done, the native homing passion of the soul for the Beyond, and has creatively developed the outreach of his nature in the God-direction. The result is that he has occasions when the larger Life with which he feels himself kin seems to surround him and answer back to his soul's quest, as a sensitized magnetic needle, if it were conscious, might feel itself enveloped by the currents that sweep back upon it from the electrical storehouse of the sun.

It is a well-known fact that a person can slowly build up a creative inner self which acquires a far-reaching selective power and so becomes a constructive factor in all important acts and decisions. The man becomes almost infallible in his sense of moral direction, in his intuition of what is right *for him*. In much the same way an artistic creator acquires a taste, an insight, a critical judgment, and, best of all, a creative power that operates almost unconsciously, and that is wellnigh infallible. Little invisible "jinnees," as Robert Louis Stevenson used to say, seem to bring ideas and plots and illustrations, and present them to the author on a golden platter. So, too, by sincerity of soul, by correspondence with intimations and openings of life and light, and by obedience to what seems to be heavenly vision, there slowly accumulates a body of inner wisdom, a clear sense of spiritual direction, and an unfailing conviction of fellowship with a Great Companion.

The moment the highest type of spiritual personality arrives, as in the case of Christ and the most consummate saints, the consciousness of God is a calm and steady, as well as a controlling feature of life. It is, as I have been saying, like the sure and infallible creative power of the supreme aesthetic geniuses. The laws and principles of art in the great geniuses seem to be native to their minds. They *see* where others grope. But somehow the beautiful objects which they create become straightway the priceless possessions of the race, and they reveal the fact that we who are of smaller stature bear nevertheless in our inner structure capacities of appreciation which fit the supreme creations of genius. So, too, the God who is the unquestioned object of reality for the greatest spiritual geniuses breaks, at least dimly, on the souls of the most ordinary of us.

There is [General J. C. Smuts writes] a subtle, profound, synthetic activity at work among our sensations and intuitions which cannot be ascribed to the ordinary conscious activities of the Mind. Is it [he asks] a far-fetched idea to assume that behind the special senses and their evolution, and *pari passu* with their evolution, *the mother sense* from which they were evolved has silently continued to grow and evolve as the binding,

uniting, cementing element among the de-
liverances of the special senses?[3]

Some such deeper *mother sense* for the value of
beauty, of love, of moral goodness, and of the infinite worth of the soul is surely operative in most
of our lives.

When we raise the question of the objectivity
of these experiences there is no easy answer. The
proof of objectivity in any field, even in that of
sense perception, has been the intellectual task of
all the centuries, and after all the coöperative
labor it is difficult to produce an argument that
is bound to convince the doubter who questions
whether the external world *is* the way it appears.
Fortunately our common sense solves the problem
for most of us. That and our practical nature
carry us forward without waiting for the slow
proofs.

In the world of values the case is somewhat
different. There is present here a private, personal aspect which does not attach, to anything
like the same degree, to objects of sense perception. My appreciation of music or of poetry has
a subjective color all its own. No one else would
feel quite at home in my inner aesthetic world.

[3] *Holism and Evolution*, p. 256.

Nor can we without much adaptation pass on to others our judgments of right and wrong or our consciousness of duty. And yet the noblest minds have always refused to admit that beauty or obligation are out and out, through and through, subjective. These experiences in some sense have their ground in the eternal nature of things, and they conform, in inner law and substance, to some overarching reality beyond us but not alien to our finite minds. It seems evident that moral practice slowly builds up a richer, deeper inner life within us and reveals a cumulative power of moral advance which indicates that something in the deepest nature of the universe *backs* a person who is making his life an organ of ethical goodness.

There is the same kind of objective evidence in the highest forms of mystical experience. There is, to begin with, a majestic *conviction of objectivity*. The mystic is sure that he has found what he has been seeking—as sure as the climber is that he has reached his peak. The sight itself is convincing. It has all the certainty that objects of sense have to the normal man. But it must be admitted that the usual verifications of our sense facts are wanting. The mystic cannot describe his object in the categories of common

speech, nor can he get the corroborative testimony of other spectators. He has seen what he
has seen, and in its first-hand quality of acquaintance it forever remains just his incommunicable
experience. That seems, no doubt, a damaging
admission and, for some, ends the debate.

But here once more, as with aesthetic and ethical experience, there comes a slow but very convincing type of verification. The life of the
person takes on new depth. There is a marked
increase in unity and coherence to the personality.
The experience brings furtherance of life-qual-
ities. The whole spiritual nature is fructified. A
typical fortification of character is wrought in
him. He not only stands the world better but
he becomes a better organ and bearer of spiritual
forces. The perfume of holiness breathes from
him. He reveals, in demonstration and power,
the attainment of qualities of life which, even
among Christian believers, are far too rare and
unusual. Mystical experiences refashion the recipient's *active attitude* toward all that constitutes life. The soul, as William James would
say, is made "more energetic." It becomes possible not only to *vote* for a larger total universe
of good, but it even becomes possible, now, in
some real sense, to make a creative contribution

to that universe of good. *That* assuredly is one kind of verification. If we cannot point to unanswerable proofs that the mystic's experience carries objective validity, yet it can be shown, I think, that it has the same marks of self-transcendence that go with the other supreme values of life—beauty, truth, love, and goodness. There is something more to it than a subjective *feel*. Lord Balfour, in the restraint of style which is usual to him, says that "aesthetic values are in part dependent upon a spiritual conception of the world in which we live."[4] It is through these values, he says in another place, that "men have obtained an authentic glimpse of a world more resplendent and not less real than that in which they tramp their daily round—a value which cannot be maintained in a merely naturalistic setting."[5]

Professor A. Stanley Eddington, one of the foremost living scientists, said in his closing Gifford Lecture in March 1927:

> Why is it that we attach so much truth and importance to the values determined by the mind, unless they are the reflection of the mind of an absolute Valuer! How can that

[4] *Theism and Humanism*, p. 87.

[5] *Ibid*, p. 82.

mystic unity with the world, experienced in exceptional moments, continue to feed the soul in the sordid routine of life, unless we can approach the World-Spirit in the midst of our cares and duties in the relationship of spirit to Spirit?

Plato, in the *Phaedo*, declared that if we are to find and verify these larger realities of life we must mount up to the region where they are to be seen. We must see them as part of an eternal order, not as a momentary flash of light in our darkness. "Anyone," he says, "dwelling in the bottom of the sea, and remaining there through sloth or weakness, would of course never reach the surface of the sea, nor would he see how much more pure and beautiful is that upper region than is the place where he is immersed." The perspective of the bird looking from the upper air, as some one has said, is vastly different from the contracted point of view of a frog on a lily-pad; and somewhat so the experience of a mystic, or the thrill of one who loves beauty, may be taken in its subjective isolation, or it may just as well be lifted up and interpreted in terms of a deeper universe which gives occasion for such experiences.

Important as the mystical element is, it would be a grave mistake to *reduce* religion to the bare basis of uninterpreted experience. We cannot have knowledge in any field without a body of observed facts, but knowledge does not consist of mere observations or experiments or empirical occurrences. It consists rather of systematic interpretation of observations and experiments and facts of experience. They are lifted up and seen in the light of the laws and principles which they exhibit.

So, too, religion in its full meaning is vastly more than flashes of insight, intuitions of a Beyond, invasions of an environing Life, convictions of a Light that never was on sea or land. Religion builds on these deep-lying intimations of the soul and would be poor without them, but there is immensely more to say before the whole truth is uttered. Religion draws upon the whole nature and all the resources of man's complete life. It is essentially bound up with all the processes of the intellect and with all the deeper issues of the will as well as with these first-hand intimations of the soul's vision. The present-day revolt from doctrine is in many ways superficial. There can be no great religion without the interpretation of life, of the universe, of experience, of mind, of God. What we ought to revolt from is traditional dogma. We ought to challenge the

elaborate logical constructions of bygone metaphysics, and base our interpretations on the sure
ground of *vital religious experience* and on the
unescapable implications of our minds as they
coöperate with a universe which reveals rationality from outermost husk to innermost core. In
insisting on *experience* I am not unmindful of the
more yet that must go with experience. It is no
lazy mysticism that we want, no vain hope that
God will give all the treasures of the Spirit "to
His beloved in sleep." I have no word of en-
couragement to offer those persons who expect
the palaces of the soul to be built and furnished
by magically rubbing an Aladdin's lamp, or by
saying over some "blessed word" like Mesopo-
tamia, or some phrase from "the *patois* of
Canaan." The religious life is of all things
strenuous business. It calls for heroic adventure.
But one of the essential aspects of religion now
and always is the experiment, made in the soul's
inner laboratory, of the personal discovery of
that more than ourselves whom we call God.

It seems to me that the time has come to stop
using the word mysticism as an alias for what is
uncanny and obscurantist. I always feel a sense
of shock when at this late date I hear a scholar
say apologetically: "Of course I do not want my

words taken as implying any sympathy with mysticism," as though such an implication would at once wreck his reputation for sanity and sound judgment. "I keep my feet on the ground; I am no mystic" is another favorite way of saying that a "mystic" is a fever-infected maker of mirages. Mysticism is not a synonym for the "mysterious." It does not mean something "occult," or "esoteric," or "gnostic," or "pseudo-psychic." It only means that the soul of man has dealings with realities of a different order from that with which senses deal. Everybody admits that this happens in some degree when we experience *beauty*, for then there is surely something present beyond what senses report. The mystic merely pushes his claim still farther and insists that his experience reveals the fact that the inner self has a spiritual environment in which it lives and moves and has its being.

NEW STUDIES IN MYSTICAL
RELIGION

NEW STUDIES IN MYSTICAL RELIGION

CHAPTER I

MYSTICAL RELIGION AND THE ABNORMAL

A TRAIL of ill health runs across the story of the lives of many mystics, and pathologists have always been ready to discount the spiritual value of mysticism by showing that it is a near neighbor to hysteria and to a great variety of emotional diseases. There is no use attempting to deny that some of the mystics of history have shown peculiar traits of constitution. Nobody can read the lives of St. Francis of Assisi, St. Catherine of Genoa, Jacob Boehme, George Fox, Madame Guyon, or St. Teresa without feeling that these extraordinary persons had crises of illness which threatened to shatter both their physical and mental health; and there are many other less famous persons of the mystical type who have at least run close up to the boundary of normality.

Some of the so-called "New Psychologists," noting that abnormal traits have appeared in certain religious founders and leaders, and generalizing prematurely from the results of psycho-analysis, have leaped to the conclusion that religion is essentially a mild form of mental disease. They assert that religion is due to a "suppression" of hard and undesirable facts of life and to a corresponding tendency to "project" emotional wishes into the field of reality. God and all the other "visions of relief," which make up the stock of religious beliefs, are built up, they claim, by similar processes to those by which a person with an "inferiority complex" finally succeeds in convincing himself that he is Alexander the Great, or Napoleon Bonaparte.

We need not be disturbed by the obvious fact that *auto-suggestion* does play an enormous rôle in human life. Sometimes it is a constructive principle and sometimes it is a "defeative" one; sometimes it is a normal function and sometimes it is an abnormal one. The word auto-suggestion merely names a process, it does not settle its significance. Whenever the soul of man travels out beyond the *fact aspect* of sense experience it is due no doubt in large measure to some native, fundamental *urge*, or *élan*, which may quite properly be called an *auto-urge*. But that in no way discredits the effects which result, any more

than human vision is discredited by the fact that
it springs from a native capacity in the retina.
The real test will in the end be the *value* of the
experience under consideration.

The claim of the "New Psychologists" that
religion is abnormal "projection" would quite obviously mean that the whole race is more or less
tainted with abnormality, and that precisely those
persons who have been the supreme exponents and
interpreters of man's highest experiences and aspirations have been most markedly abnormal.
Under those circumstances, many of us would prefer, I think, to line up and take our place among
the "abnormals," as in most respects they have
been the finest specimens of the race. I have long
felt that we have among us a school of theorists
who tend to "project" abnormality into everything, and who have a "complex" for discovering
"complexes." Some psychologists need psycho-
therapeutic treatment as much as some of our re-
ligionists do!

Rudolf Otto, in his *Das Heilige*, is, I am convinced, much closer to the truth of things when
he treats the essential aspect of religion as a
hushed, trembling, palpitant response of the human soul in the presence of august, majestic, mysterious, awe-inspiring realities, which produce a

consciousness of what he calls the "numinous."
His word is from the Latin *numen*, and stands for
anything that transcends the finite, the known, the
naturalistic, and the describable, and which moves
us with awe. A "numinous" experience is unique,
different from any other experience, *sui generis*
and irreducible. It introduces a new *quality* to
life. It is an original capacity of the total self,
and is as inexplicable in terms of anything else
as is appreciation of beauty, or the love of music,
or the capacity for mathematics, or the sense of
moral obligation, or the necessity we feel to pre-
suppose a cause for an effect. All these unique
traits in us defy analysis. They belong to our
"deeper nature" as persons. They can no more
be "explained" than we can explain that peculiar
quality which we call the taste of "sweetness," or
the color of "redness." You either have it or
you do not have it, and if you do not have it then
there is no use arguing. One takes his dog to the
art gallery in vain, and one labors to no purpose
to interpret the meaning of "ought" to a person
who has never got beyond utilitarian morality. If
nothing ever stirs a person's soul with hushed awe,
if nothing ever makes him vibrant and palpitant
because he feels himself in the presence of the
in-breaking of the Divine, the "numinous," then

there is no way to make that person comprehend what we mean by the essential aspect of religion. It cannot be conveyed by a "detour" route—it must come into consciousness direct and first-hand. The person who possessed no capacity to feel the "numinous" aspect would, according to Professor Otto, be defective and abnormal. The religious capacity is something belonging to the fundamental nature of the soul which is set into characteristic activity by those exalted situations and occasions that let the Divine break into consciousness. This first-hand "numinous" state of mind may very well be the basis of what is called mystical religion.

Something of that same sort is what Auguste Sabatier meant when he said: "I am religious because I cannot help it. It is a moral necessity of my being. . . . The necessity which I experience in my individual life I find to be still more invincible in the collective life of humanity. Humanity is not less incurably religious than I am." The great Frenchman then proceeds to characterize religion as that inward happy crisis by which human life is transformed and the gates within one's being are opened toward the ideal life. "All human development springs from it and ends in it." "Man is not; he has to make

himself"—and religion is essentially the inner
energy by which the spiritual creation is wrought.

George Santayana, in a charming essay on
"Platonic Love," defines religion as the "passion-
ate pursuit of something permanent in a world of
change, of something absolute in a world of rela-
tivity." With his usual touches of beauty of style,
he comments on those "visitations from a better
world" which all of us at moments have had, and
then he goes on to say that the pursuit of this
eternal good

> Gives our lives whatever they have of true
> earnestness and meaning and the approach
> to it whatever they have of joy. So far is
> this ideal, Plato would say, from being an
> illusion, that it is the source of the world,
> the power that keeps us in existence. But
> for it we should be dead. . . . We, and the
> whole universe, exist only by the passionate
> attempt to return to our perfection, by the
> radical need of losing ourselves in God!
> That ineffable good is our natural posses-
> sion; all we honor in this life is but the par-
> tial recovery of our birthright; every de-
> lightful thing is like a rift in the clouds
> through which we catch a glimpse of our na-
> tive heaven. If that heaven seems so far

away and the idea of it so dim and unreal, it is because we are so far from self-knowledge, so much immersed in what is alien and destructive to the soul.

Francis Thompson has expressed this same idea in his well-known lines:

> 'Tis ye, 'tis your estrangéd faces
> That miss the many-splendoured thing.

Here, then, in these three healthy-minded philosophers—one German, one French, and one cosmopolitan—we have an alternative to the theory that religion in its essential nature is disease. They all three, from very different approaches and with widely differing individual interpretations, find religion to be due to the inherent constitution of man's fundamental nature as a person, and at the same time, to the fact that there is Something in the eternal nature of the universe which breaks in upon man's inner life, disturbs his lethargy, and calls him forward to realize his destiny. Some such presupposition underlies all my interpretations of religion.

I have so far been using the word religion somewhat loosely. It is a word of a thousand meanings, and if we are to make any progress in our valuation of it, we must be more specific in the differentiation of the type with which we are to deal. I am concerned for the moment with mystical religion which I here define as an overbrimming experience of contact, fellowship, or even union with a larger Life which impinges on our own life.

If we are seriously to claim that there is a type of religion which thus reveals God and man as conterminous or conjunct, we must show some ground for thinking that God is a God who breaks through the veils and framework of the world and manifests Himself *here*; and at the same time we must have some evidence that there are valid human experiences of correspondence and fellowship with the Divine. It has become very clear to all who work in the fields of science and philosophy that the visible world has come out of an invisible one; in fact, the real timber out of which the world is built is invisible timber. It seems probable, too, that the temporal has come out of and has its deeper being in something eternal. One reason for thinking so is the unescapable fact that the visible and temporal world always turns out to be a fragment—never a self-contained and self-explanatory whole. What is here implies and involves *more*. There is always and everywhere an *overplus*—something which must be presup-

posed. Our method of explaining by causes only
carries us back in unending regress, in which we
never find an adequate "real cause." We find ourselves in the same dilemma as the Indian who said
that the earth rested for support on a tortoise,
and the tortoise on an elephant. And the elephant? He must stand on another elephant, and
then there must be elephants all the way down!
Plato and Aristotle are taking the only adequate
course for sound thinking when they insist that
the order and the purposeful "forms" of the
world must come from an intelligent Mind that
underlies and yet transcends all that appears.

We have come to see that creation is not confined to a few days at the "beginning." Every
day is a day of creation as much as the first day
ever was. The new continues to emerge, and the
cosmic order proves to be a growing thing. The
universe is in the main a one-way street—it is
going forward, not backward. The "mutations"
which mark its upward progress are an "over-
plus" beyond what was here before. They
"emerge," or "break in," or, as Tennyson would
put it, they "draw from out the boundless deep."
In a great emotional passage, Macbeth calls the
visible world, "this bank and shoal of time"; that
is to say, it is a tiny island surrounded by a vaster

world of reality, somewhat as the Pacific Ocean pours around a coral reef which has come up out of its deeps.

F.W.H. Myers, after years of patient research and investigation, announced his central faith in these bold words:

> There exists around us a spiritual universe and that universe is in actual relation with the material (universe). From the spiritual universe comes the energy which maintains the material, the energy which makes the life of each individual spiritual. Our spirits are supported by a perpetual indrawing of this energy and the vigor of that indrawal is perpetually changing, much as the vigor of our absorption of material nutriment changes from hour to hour.

One of the oddest things about the universe is the way in which it fits and correlates with our tiny, finite minds. Our mathematics is precisely the same as the mathematics of the great world, the macrocosm. Everything "out there" conforms to our mental geometry and must in some way belong to the same mental system. We can discover a new planet before we have found it. We can calculate its locus and it must be there! We can forecast a new element by the laws of atoms and then by experiment proceed to find it. There is some kind of higher correlation and foundational connection between our minds and the cosmic order.

The beauty with which the world is filled is an extraordinary overplus above and beyond the utilitarian aspect. It is not found or accounted for by any casual explanation of things. Mechanism gives us efficiency and utility, but it does not give us beauty. Beauty does not come under categories of space, or matter, or quantity, though it breaks through space and matter and quantities. It is something superadded to our world of fact, and law and cause. It emerges as soon as there is a beholder who can bring a certain type of mind into correspondence with this overbrimming feature of the world. In every case where beauty is felt, whether through eye or ear or any other sense, consciousness is fused, integrated, and *en rapport* with its object as it never is while it is merely dealing with the object as a bare *fact*. Something has happened now that is supertemporal and super-spatial, and that defies complete analysis. To deal with it analytically is to miss it and to lose it.

History—I mean the historical process—is once more something which cannot be reduced to a rigid causal series. There is a significant over-plus—something overbrimming boils over and inundates the cold facts of history. It is a dramatic movement. It is full of surprises. It has a *meaning* which can be interpreted like a cumulative story or a work of art. It reveals and it verifies moral principles. It is not merely wild and fortuitous. It is not a series of "repeatable" events. One act prepares for the next. The new continuously correlates with the old. It has its laws and rational order. But ever and anon persons of genius, or persons possessed of a unique dynamic quality, appear with some novel and unpredictable ideal which affects not only their own destiny but which, at the same time, alters the entire course of history and shifts the line of march of the whole race. Here once more the mind in us seems to correlate with and to be in correspondence with a deeper, foundational Mind that steers the majestic fleet of the ages. The moral nature revealed in us, and revealed in august fashion in the slow judgment days of history, implies and involves a deeper eternal moral nature of things, creatively operative in the fabric of life and history.

It seems consonant with all we find and with all we know to interpret this deeper foundational

World—*the noumenal world* of both Plato and Kant—as intelligent and purposeful Spirit. We ourselves are spirit, and we are, therefore, not turning away to something alien and foreign to ourselves when we talk of Spirit. *We* exhibit reason in thought and action. We transcend whatever we are dealing with and are always persons with idealizing capacity. We enjoy creating and we live under a sense of obligation toward what ought to be. We love beauty and truth and goodness, and we may well suppose that the deeper Spirit from whom we have emerged is possessed of all those traits which are highest and most beautiful in us—and more. He *is* what we are striving to be, and at the same time He transcends all that *has been and is*. *He is the guarantor of what is to be.*

But I am especially concerned now with the testimony of the human soul to the fact that there is some kind of *correspondence* with this deeper Spirit from whom we have come. We have intimations in our human nature of faculties and powers which stretch far beyond what is required for physical "survival," or for coherent correspondence with our present environment in a world of space. It seems odd that we should have hungers for something purely illusory, that we should be forever seeking for a goal that has no foundation in reality, that we should have thoughts and hopes that are loftier and nobler than the truth of things; that we should have the structure and apparatus for living in a world of spirit which, however, does not exist!

Besides all this, there are numerous persons who are conscious of some sort of commerce and fellowship with a much larger environment than this visible and tangible one. The experiences of this type are various and variable. The most common experiences come as invasions or in-rushes. It seems on these occasions as though a larger and fuller Life flooded in and connected the recipient with what is essential for his spiritual life, somewhat as the red corpuscles in the blood connect us with the oxygen which keeps our life going. Once at sea, in the middle of the night, when all unbeknown to me then my little boy, left behind in America, was dying, with no father by him to hold his hand, I suddenly felt myself surrounded by a mighty presence and held as though by invisible arms. At no other time in my life have I ever felt such positive contact, and on this occasion my entire being was calmed, and I was inwardly prepared to meet the message of sorrow which waited for me next day when I landed at Liverpool. It may be said, no doubt, that this and all such experiences are only intuitive flashes from one's own submerged deposits of memory, imagination, and emotion. I can only answer, yes, it may be so; but it may also be true as well that in such moments, when the inner self is unified and heightened in its powers of apprehension, some real influx of life and energy from beyond the margins of our own being may break in and find us.

There is frequently—usually, I think I may say—a feeling of objective presence, a sense of reality, almost, or quite, on a par with what goes with the perceptions of our particular senses. Sometimes it is vague, inarticulate, and haunting rather than intense and specific. Sometimes there is a sudden increase of vitality, of moral earnestness, of faith and conviction. There is a fine and well-known passage from Plotinus which beautifully describes what I mean:

Oftentimes when I awake out of the slumber of the body and come to a realizing sense of myself, and retiring from the world outside, give myself up to inward contemplation, I behold a wonderful beauty. I believe then that I belong to a higher and better world and I strive to develop within me a glorious life and to become one with the Godhead. And by this means I receive such an energy of life that I rise above the world of things.

Sometimes, especially in moments of intense prayer and communion, there comes a remarkable sense of answer and response. Praying ceases to be a one-sided activity and passes over into an experience of what Clement of Alexandria called "mutual and reciprocal correspondence." A circuit suddenly closes and the Below and Above find each other as the two electrodes do the moment they both touch earth, no matter how much space intervenes. This feeling of answering presence, this sense of correspondence, reaches its height in group silence, when many earnest worshipers coöperate, in unity of spirit and harmony of purpose, to become a fused and living organ of the Spirit.

> A sound is heard
> As of a mighty wind, and men devout,
> Strangers of Rome and the new proselytes,
> In their own tongue hear Thy wondrous word.

More often, however, the effect of correspondence with God is revealed in practical activity rather than as something clearly registered in consciousness. Many persons practice the presence of God although they have no momentous experiences of invasion and though they could not say positively that they have ever felt the circuit close. They feel themselves helped to bear the burdens of life; they feel led, impelled, and guided in difficult emergencies; they have quiet strength supplied for tasks that ought to be done; visions of service open before them; grace is showered down upon them; and "kindly light" shines on the path they tread. No one dazzling light, perhaps, ever breaks in, like the Damascus vision, but a thousand starlike illuminations fill their sky and they live a high-powered life because they are all the time recipients and transmitters of spiritual energies from beyond themselves.

There is a very striking passage in Sir Ernest Shackleton's account of his terrific Antarctic experiences in the volume entitled *South*. His ship was lost in an ice-jam. He and his men floated on the ice for eight months, the latter part of the time in constant peril by the disintegration of the ice-floe. At last they took to open boats and finally landed on the bleak, inhospitable shores of Elephant Island, where no man's foot had ever been. Leaving twenty-two of his men there, he made his way with five others in a small boat eight hundred miles across one of the worst of seas, to

South Georgia, landing on the wrong side of the island and being compelled to cross, with two other men, a mountain range covered with glacier ice that seemed impassable. In his quiet style of speech, the great explorer says:

I know that during that long and racking march of thirty-six hours over the unnamed mountains and glaciers of South Georgia, *it seemed to me often that we were four, not three*. I said nothing to my companions on this point, but afterwards Worsley said to me, "Boss, I had a curious feeling on the march that there was another person with us." Crean (the third man) confessed to the same idea. One feels the dearth of human words, the roughness of mortal speech in trying to describe things intangible, but a record of our journey would be incomplete without a reference to a subject very near to our hearts.

There is, too, the powerful testimony of inward peace which many a soul knows, even though no special claim of mystical experience is made. This is not just absence of tension, strain, worry, turmoil, bustle, and hurry. The Greeks called that state of mind "ataraxy." It is a negative word. It means *freedom from* something. Mys-

tical peace is a glorious, positive, and affirmative
word. It is inward order, calm, control, confidence, joy, power, blessedness even in the midst
of outward pain, difficulty, loss, defeat, frustra-
tion, and complexity. Strength from somewhere
is added to the native stock of endurance; a power
not one's own flows in; and, suddenly, the feeble
and timid soul can stand the universe, garrisoned
thus with a peace that overpasses comprehension.

There are, besides these milder forms of correspondence, certain types of experience of a
more extreme sort, reaching the apex in trance
and ecstasy. Some authorities incline to the view
that no experience short of ecstasy should be
called mystical. A mystical experience for them
is one which transcends consciousness, has no content, focuses on nothing, is a unification so complete that all difference, otherness, concreteness
vanish in a blank, abstract *one*. I see no reason
for this extreme view. It is true, no doubt, that
many great mystics of history have looked upon
this attainment of an experience super-everything
known, seen, felt, thought, or desired, as the mystical experience *par excellence*. "In one trembling
flash," St. Augustine felt that he arrived at That
Which Is, the Absolute, Self-same One. It fits
the Greek tradition from Plotinus onward to

glorify the apprehension of the Abstract and, therefore, any experience which terminates in a "pure" beholding of Nothing-in-particular seems to be an exalted attainment.

Sometimes it probably is. There can be an exalted state of undifferentiated consciousness, like that which marks the highest moments of joy in music, or of visible beauty, or of the spell of pure mathematics, when without thinking of anything in particular one has an attitude of wonder and feels all the forces of the inner life raised to their maximum degree. The poets and the creative musicians have much to say of these occasions; and, though neither poet nor musician, I have felt that spell at Mürren before the Jungfrau, in Dresden before the Sistine Madonna, on the Mount of Olives at sunset, at the Grand Canyon of the Colorado, and in Chartres Cathedral. What happens in the presence of sights and sounds and perhaps sometimes from odors may also happen to gifted persons when they are swept from within with a sense of God, or become suddenly aware of the eternal Lover of their soul. The experience, as such, betokens no sign of abnormality, and might easily be the mark of the most perfect health—in fact, there is no health quite to compare with this glow and tingle of spirit.

The fact remains, however, and will not down, that trance and ecstasy are not normal states of life, and furthermore that the biographies of mystics are heavily freighted with details of what must be pronounced to be abnormality. I have insisted that a consciousness which has no concrete content may not necessarily be abnormal, but at the same time an unfocused mind gazing with "no speculation" in the eyes, seeing nothing, thinking nothing, remembering nothing, and yet believing that the nothing is All, that zero is infinity, can with difficulty be distinguished from diseased imagination. If mysticism were nothing but a series of trances or ecstatic states, it would surely be a doubtful asset for religion, and we should be hanging our spiritual hopes on a flimsy cable.

It would appear that the highest contributions to life have been made to the world by persons of mobile, fluent, slightly unstable mental organization, capable of quick modification, sensitive to subtle influences which tougher organizations miss, nerves in hair-trigger condition, and mind almost magically responsive to marginal suggestions. Inward shifts of scene come as easily as

they do in a kaleidoscope; a slight turn and the
entire scenery of life has altered. The genius in
any field must have a peculiar structure and one
that entails risks and liabilities.

> The earth must richer sap secrete,
>   (Could ye in time but know it!)
> Must juice concrete with fiercer heat,
>   Ere she can make her poet.
>
>   .   .   .   .
>
> Her cheaper broods in palaces
>   She raises under glasses,
> But souls like these, heav'n's hostages,
>   Spring shelterless as grasses:
> They share earth's blessing and her bane,
>   The common sun and shower;
> What makes your pain to them is gain,
>   Your weakness is their power.
>
> These larger hearts must feel the rolls
>   Of stormier-waved temptation;
> These star-wide souls between their poles
>   Bear zones of tropic passion.

Geniuses are, in our human order, something
like the "mutation" in the biological order. They
are unpredictable and they are variants. They
reach forward and introduce something that was
not here before, something that could break in
only through them, but they pay a price for their

uniqueness. They not only "bear zones of tropic passion," but they live near the perilous edge of instability. The line between the normal and the abnormal is hard to draw in their case—it is often wavy. That very trait in their nature, which makes revelation possible through them, also makes dissociation equally possible.

It is not only in the biographies of mystics that we find the trail of abnormality; it is incident to the psychological structure of this sort of extreme type. The mystic has, no doubt, sometimes striven for trance and ecstasy as a spiritual goal, just as early Christians strove to "speak with tongues" as a proof of the gift of the Spirit. But the wisest mystics have usually been aware of the fact that the training and culture of the soul to become an organ for God in the world is vastly more important than the attainment of a nirvana state of mind can be. They were untrained in psychology—no Freud, no "New Psychologists," had instructed them! They often made sad blunders. Their very way of life increased their natural tendency to instability. Then, too, their disciples, admirers, and biographers strained after the marvelous. But we know now that the noteworthy facts in their lives were not the ecstasies, the stigmata, the levitations, the burning

heat in the heart, the telepathies, and the automatisms. These are the signs and sequels of their
fluently and unstably organized systems. The
great traits are the ones upon which they themselves laid the main stress. They were the recipients of a surge of conviction that they had found
God. They were the bringers and bearers of
fresh insight and vision of God's spiritual nature
and character. They raised human love and loyalty to God's will to a unique height of intensity,
and they fused their love and loyalty with a joy
and rapture seldom found in religion. They, for
the most part, exhibited a unique degree of moral
earnestness and passion with a rare acuteness of
conscience and a unique purity of life. They were
tremendous transmitters of energy. Their im-
pact and momentum were extraordinary. They
championed   causes,   organized   movements,
founded societies, reformed the Church, led cru-
sades, and took their part in rebuilding the world
of their time. Their conviction made their words
weigh and their lives count—and what they *saw*
with their inner spirits they forged into deeds or
wove into the fabric of life, and proved that the
eternal nature of things backed their souls' vision.

But the outstanding trait of the mystic is his
discovery that religion—the experience of God—

is an absolute value, an all-sufficient end in itself.
That does not mean that thrills of beatific vision
constitute his religion, or that

> It is engender'd in the eyes,
> With gazing fed.

Mystical religion is satisfied with nothing short of
complete spiritual health and fortification for
energetic living.   The healing of the wounds of
sin is the first business, but the complete process
of the soul includes the formation of inward purity, gentleness, grace, control, coherence, unification, dedication, and a love that knows no boundaries.

The mystic has a constitution which by nature
is in danger of disintegration and dissociation.
He is threatened with excessive centrifugal tendencies.   Parts of his being incline to run off
and do business on their own hook.   It is essential
for him, therefore, to become *integrated*, knit up
into a coherent whole.   Just that work of unification is what is usually wrought by his discovery
of God.   His mighty conviction tends to bind his
life into a well-organized system.   The divided
self becomes unified.   George Fox is an excellent
illustration of the cohesive power of a great experience of God.   It turned his darkness into

light, his sadness into joy, his despair into hope, and under its influence his poor distraught mind seized upon and held to a constructive central purpose. At the same time, the whole creation seemed to him to be transfigured, "new-molded," and penetrated with a "new smell."

Not less remarkable than this integrating force is the birth in the soul of a love which rises above all self-interest. It is a love which seems in very truth to be "born of God." It is very patient, very kind. It is not provoked. It endures all things. It abides when everything else fails. It goes on loving in the face of scorn and misunderstanding. It outlives strife and wrath. It wearies out pride and cruelty. It takes its kingdom with entreaty, not with contention. It believes and hopes even when all the stars are hidden. It goes all the way to find and to win and to save.

> Love looked down and beheld hatred
> "Thither will I go," said Love.

Such love as that is, of course, not necessarily confined to mystics. It is prescribed by Christ and by St. Paul as the mark and badge of all Christians. "You are to love," the great Galilean said, "even as I have loved you." Only, it must be said, such love does not often come to consummation in any

person until that person has found and felt the
love of God in a great first-hand experience of the
mystical type.   It is Love that begets love—we
love because He first loved.   Most Christian
mystics would join with St. Paul in saying, "the
love of Christ constrains me."

What the mystic will do with his life after he
has *seen*, after he has been *organized and fortified* and has been *made a lover*, we need not stop
to ask.   It will depend on what is specifically there
to be done in his day and generation.   But we
can take it for settled that he will be a hundred-
horsepower person in his world.

What I want to come back to is my previous
contention that the mystic holds religion to be an
end in itself.   He is not trying to find God in
order to use Him, and when he finds Him he does
not think of Him as a handy utility.   There are
some things in this universe, like the beauty of
Emerson's "Rhodora," which are their "own ex-
cuse for being."   Men have sought for God
mainly so that they might have a First Cause for
motion and for the vast congeries of things.
They have searched for Him so that they might
have some one to rescue them from the perils of
an unseen world.   In all this seeking and searching, men have persisted in their selfishness and

have held tenaciously to their ego-focus. It will not do. After winning that kind of salvation, we still need to be saved from our poor utilitarian religion. "Two loves have built two cities," St. Augustine wrote while the Roman Empire was toppling around him. "The love of self reaching on to the contempt of God has built the city of the world; the love of God reaching on to the contempt of self has built the city of God. Let everyone inquire of himself what he loveth; and he shall resolve himself of whence he is a citizen."

We must not ask religion to furnish us with ready-made answers to our intellectual problems. They are to be solved only by the mind that has raised them. We must not expect religion to give back-door secret information about the future of the soul. We must take religion for what it intrinsically is, a way of correspondence with God, a source of spiritual energy, a spring of joy, a burst of inspiration, an organizing power, the begetter of undying love. It is one of those overbrimming realities—beyond the mechanical order of things—which is good not because we can cash it in and use it, but because it is good in itself, its own sweet reason for being. "No soul is rested," wrote Lady Julian of Norwich, "until it be *noughted* of all that is made"—and for her, the way of "noughting" is the way of love, loving not to get something but only to love.

If one sets out to prove that every trait is abnormal which does not have utilitarian value, which does not aid survival or promote egoistic advantage, then, of course, mystical religion, as I have interpreted it, is in that light "abnormal." But so also on the same count are *all* intrinsic values. Beauty and truth and goodness and love, except in so far as they can be used as means, become subtle forms of disease, which realistic writers and commercialized movies know only too well how to cure! We may discount all such mental diagnosis and go on our way in peace and joy, knowing that our universe overfloods at many points and in diverse manners, and that we ourselves have inner spirits which cannot be sounded with the plummet of the utilitarian nor meted out by the measuring rod of the materialist. "Man," said St. Augustine, "is a great deep, and the hairs of his head are more easily to be numbered than the feelings and beatings of his *heart*."

CHAPTER II

MYSTICISM AND ASCETICISM

OF all the strange and baffling traits of this mysterious human life of ours, nothing is stranger than the persistent tendency which men have shown to suffer self-inflicted pain. We are sufficiently perplexed that life should be so heavily laden with unescapable natural suffering to which flesh is heir, and that man's inhumanity to man should have added on top of that another load of woes; but who would have dreamed that, besides all this, man would ingeniously invent tortures and torments of his own devising to heap upon himself? So, however, it has been in all generations. Bernard Shaw has whimsically reminded us that men and women have usually assumed that they were the most moral and religious "when they were the most uncomfortable"! This tendency of man to make himself *uncomfortable for religious and moral ends* is what we mean by asceticism.

There are many reasons why ascetic practices

have been and still are adopted. In the early primitive stages of life, such practices were often enjoined by tribal custom to serve as ordeals and methods of discipline for purposes of forming a stern and hardy race, capable of facing the most heroic tasks for the welfare of the tribe. If a boy was to become an enduring warrior and make his contribution to the daring achievements of his people, it seemed natural for him to undergo, at some crisis of his youth, a painful initiation into the corporate life of the tribe, and as the tribe and the god of the tribe were closely identified, this self-accepted suffering took on a religious meaning. Once baptized with the sanction of tribal custom, self-inflicted pain rose in importance and significance and often tended to become an end in itself, especially with individuals who were morbid-minded.

Then, again, every person who is dedicated to any serious undertaking discovers that he must make sacrifices for the pursuit which absorbs him. The universe has many levels and we find ourselves confronted with a rivalry of aims. No one can plan the affairs of an empire, or discover a new law of nature, or write an epoch-making book, or create an immortal work of art without cutting away and killing off a large number of live and appealing human interests. Dante's divine poem, he tells us, made him "lean for years." So, too, every affirmation of a great life-purpose involves the negation of many things which one might have chosen had they not been incompatible with the central aim. The athlete of the spirit, as well as the athlete of the stadium, must practice self-restraint and refuse to take easy lines of least resistance. "To scorn delights and live laborious days" seems as natural as breathing to those who have found an aim worthy of the sacrifice. There is a way of life for which it is not too much to pluck out an eye which hinders or to cut off a right arm if it hampers the onward course. This will perhaps hardly be called asceticism, but in any case it helps us to see how natural sacrifice and self-inflicted pain may be.

Love is beyond question one of the most powerful springs of self-sacrifice. The course of true love, in more senses than one, never runs smooth. It is a perilous way to take if one wishes only to play safe and be comfortable. I am not now talking about love as a sensuous passion, the love that arises through "a return to nature." I am thinking of that higher form of love in which the natural instincts and emotions have been "sublimated" by the operation of ideal influences and

spiritual aims, as happens whenever love is at its
noblest. Love is thus one of our greatest spiritual creations. To love deeply and truly involves sharing the agonies and tragedies of the
beloved one's life as well as the peace and joys
of it. There are no sufferings like the sufferings
which a loving heart must endure when the one
who is loved goes wrong and takes a course which
threatens to destroy his nobler nature and his
higher possibilities. The deepest and holiest trait
of our human nature, our capacity for unselfish
love that will not let go, is at the same time the
source of our profoundest suffering and the greatest of all our sacrificial spurs.

A modern poet has very nobly and beautifully
expressed the cost which love entails:

If love should count you worthy, and should deign
    One day to seek your door and be your guest,
    Pause! ere you draw the bolt and bid him rest,
If in your old content you would remain;
For not alone he enters; in his train
    Are angels of the mist, the lonely quest,
    Dreams of the unfulfilled and unpossessed,
And sorrow, and Life's immemorial pain.
He wakes desires you never may forget,
    He shows you stars you never saw before,
    He makes you share with him forevermore

The burden of the world's divine regret.
How wise you were to open not! and yet
    How poor if you should turn him from the door![1]

But here, once more, it is hardly psychologically sound to call "ascetic" the sacrifices which are made for love's sake. They become "second-nature" actions. They seem as normal and natural as our other great springs of life. One says as, out of pure love, he walks the way of the Cross, "How otherwise?"

The largest sum of ascetic suffering is, however, probably due to the stern requirements of some more or less abstract theory. It is amazing with what dynamic consequences certain abstract theories are loaded. William James used to contend that "abstract conceptions" are notoriously weak in impulsive power. Sometimes they are weak and sometimes they are not. It depends altogether on *what* abstract conception is at issue. Men have faced death in its most terrible forms, have starved every appetite, have surrendered every precious possession, have lain long weary years in darkness and dungeon for an abstract conception, for nothing but the remote implica-

[1] S. R. Lysaght, *Poems of the Unknown Way.*

tions of a theory which was constructed out of logic.

One of the theories which has most often produced ascetic practices has been the dualistic theory that matter, by its essential nature, is evil. If matter is evil, then of course the body is evil, and all its propensities are tainted and tinctured with evil. The very act of propagating life is assumed to be sinful, for it dooms another spirit to enter the prison-house of gross flesh and compels it to be subjected to constant contact with this defiling substance. This theory, therefore, has seemed to many to enjoin celibacy and virginity. With many others, who were either not as sternly rigorous, or perhaps not as scrupulously consistent, this theory of matter has not been pushed to such extreme limits, but it has, nevertheless, made *this* world seem an alien and foreign land, a world of corruption and contamination; a world, in fact, to be shunned and to be escaped from. Natural appetites, instinctive impulses, tendencies which minister to pleasure, have been regarded with suspicion or with positive disapproval. Mortification of the flesh, harsh self-denial, discipline, restraint, destruction of desire, crucifixion of the self have always been practiced wherever this theory of matter has held sway. Periods of fasting, rules of abstinence, a policy of ruthless rigor toward the body, have always accompanied this conception. What a grip this dualistic doctrine has held on the race! What a spell and fascination it has worked upon human thought!

Closely akin to this theory of matter comes a more subtle and refined theory which has had a long and dignified history—I mean the theory that the real, the true, the spiritual, is yonder in another sphere and this world is only appearance, only finite seeming, only temporal and passing show. All that is true and good and real and spiritual is beyond this poor vale of mutability. Even the beauty-loving, life-enjoying Greek came under the spell of this theory. Pythagoras, Parmenides, Plato, Plotinus, and their numerous disciples and schools, in varying degrees, gave currency to the view that the fleeting, shifting, changing things of earth are show and shadow, dim reflections seen in the caves of sense. The *truly real* is beyond in another realm and can be found only by those who turn away from the finite and temporal and learn to apprehend *that which is* in its eternal being.

It is doubtful if any more persistent and august interpretation of life has been made than this one. It is so ancient that its origin is lost in the mists of the early dawn of history. As far back as the written language of India can carry us, we find this view prevailing.

This interpretation of life breaks through the myths of many early races. It was taught in the drama-plays of the primitive Orphic mysteries. It is a common note in early poetry and philosophy. It colors all the web of Gnostic speculation. It is the one idea common to all the types of thought and religion which centered in that strange cosmopolitan Alexandria at the mouth of the Nile—Numenius, Philo, Ammonius, Clement, Origen, Plotinus, Athanasius, and Hypatia. If one comes under the sway of such a view of life, obviously the practical consequences are bound to be immensely important. It proposes, like Elijah at Carmel, a severe selection. One must choose where his chief interest is to lie. If one has the good fortune to catch a clear sight of the pearl of great price yonder, he will henceforth esteem lightly the poor tinsel things for which others drudge. He will no longer mistake street-lamps for celestial luminaries.

This view of life, then, has called multitudes to turn away from ease and comfort and to set their feet upon the *via dolorosa*. It is a question whether any other theory of life has been so

blood-red with suffering and sacrifice as this one
has been. It has entailed and enjoined every
known type of renunciation. Evelyn Underhill
asks what must be the first step of our pilgrimage back to our "real home," and her answer is:

> Clearly, a getting rid of all those elements
> of normal experience which are not in har-
> mony with reality; of illusion, evil, imper-
> fection of every kind. By false desires and
> false thoughts, man has built up for himself
> a false universe: as a mollusc, by the deliber-
> ate and persistent absorption of lime and
> rejection of all else, can build up for itself a
> hard shell which shuts it from the external
> world, and only represents in a distorted and
> unrecognizable form the ocean from which
> it was obtained. This hard and wholly un-
> nutritious shell, this one-sided secretion of
> the surface-consciousness, makes, as it were,
> a little cave of illusion for each separate
> soul. A literal and deliberate getting out of
> the cave must be for every mystic, as it was
> for Plato's prisoners, the first step in the in-
> dividual hunt for reality.[2]

In India the doctrine of *Karma* and rebirth
led quite naturally to a peculiar form of asceti-

[2] *Mysticism* p. 240.

cism. According to this doctrine of *Karma*, a man's body, his character, his disposition, gifts and temperament, his birth, wealth and station, his happiness or his sorrow in life, were all the result and just retribution for deeds and actions done in a previous incarnation. Life is expiation for the past, and at the same time determines the *Karma* of a future life.

It seemed wisest, therefore, to gain *release* from the necessity of rebirth by turning entirely away from this world of unreality and *maya* and to enter into the one, actionless Reality. Under the sway of this doctrine the consistently religious person was bound to be ascetic.

Sister Nivedita has drawn a graphic picture of the inherent asceticism of India, incarnate in the god Shiva, the great ascetic who sits absorbed in meditation, passionless and immovable. When one sees deep enough into the eternal nature of things, she declares,

> All the manifold satisfactions of the flesh become a burden. Home and kindred and intercourse with the world become a bondage. Food and sleep and the necessities of the physical life seem indifferent or intolerable. And so it comes that the Great God of the Hindu imagination is a beggar. Cov-

ered with the ashes of His sacrificial fire, so
that He is white like snow, His hair growing
untended in large masses, oblivious of cold
and heat, silent, remote from men, He sits
absorbed in eternal meditation.

Here, once more, we are in the grip not of actual
experience but of a constructed *theory* of life.

I shall speak of only one more theory under the
logic of which men have voluntarily borne heavier
burdens than those imposed by the taskmasters of
the Pharaohs. They have scourged themselves,
starved themselves, worn girdles with sharp
brads, slept on beds of torture among noisome
insects, lived on the top of lonely pillars, killed
out every propensity that pushed toward ease or
pleasure, and have succeeded in reversing that
first law of physical life—*self-preservation*. This
is the theory that God grants mercy and favors
only to those who conform to the stern conditions of the majestic sovereign of the universe,
only to those who satisfy his sense of "justice,"
only to those, in fact, who accumulate sufficient
"merit" to deserve attention. God is thought to
be imperial, severe, cold, hard, and authoritative,
and he listens only to the appeal of those who
abjectly crawl to the foot of his throne on bleed-
ing knees and who show that they have attained

a humility which is stripped of all pride, self-assertion, and human claims. Browning has drawn a vivid and living picture of this view of God in his "Caliban upon Setebos." Caliban is a type of primitive man reflecting upon the nature of his god. Caliban says of Setebos:

> The best way to escape his ire
> Is, not to seem too happy.

Therefore, Caliban "mainly dances on dark nights," "moans in the sun," "gets under holes to laugh," "never speaks his mind" except when he is in a place of safety. He proceeds:

If He caught me here,
O'erheard this speech, and asked "What chucklest at?"
'Would, to appease Him, cut a finger off,
Or of my three kid yearlings burn the best,
Or let the toothsome apples rot on tree,
Or push my tame beast for the orc to taste:
While myself lit a fire, and made a song
And sung it, *"What I hate be consecrate*
To celebrate Thee and Thy state, no mate
For Thee; what see for envy in poor me?"

Then when a sudden danger appears which seems to indicate that Setebos has heard, seen, and is angry, Caliban cries:

Lo! 'Lieth flat and loveth Setebos!
'Maketh his teeth meet through his upper lip,
Will let those quails fly, will not eat this month
One little mess of whelks, so he may 'scape!

Browning uses as the text of this poem the significant words of Scripture: "Thou thoughtest that I was altogether such an one as thyself." That is a key to much of this black theology. Men with low aims of life, with mean standards of human relationship, and with cruel instincts and passions have conceived of God as like themselves and have pictured a deity who had the character of a feudal baron. This is all a pitiful story of perversion, and we can only hope that as we learn to know the God and Father of Jesus Christ, which we are slow to do, such thoughts of God will vanish as mist before the sunrise.

Along with this perverted thought of God may be linked the equally tragic contribution which has been made to human woe by persons suffering from morbid diseases of the mind. Psychopathic persons are not confined to any age or land. They are, no doubt, produced in large numbers by the drive and strain of our strenuous and complicated civilization, but they were a feature, too, of earlier and simpler civilizations. Christ found them both in the cities and in the lonely wilds of

Palestine. Depression, self-depreciation, hate of life and joy are common features of such diseases. The subject is a sluiceway for suggestion, and when an idea once obsesses him he acts upon it. Hermit-dwellers, pillar-saints, flagellants, monks with ingenuities of torture, have often been victims, not of a logical theory, but rather, victims of insane suggestions; and their obsessions have frequently worked like a hypnotic spell upon their suggestible fellows. We have, therefore, in the long list of self-tortures, not only the many varieties of ascetic practice built on logical theories, but many more which have sprung from unsound and unstable states of mind and will.

This brief review of ascetism should make clear the fact that it has attached to every form and type of religious faith, and is not the exclusive characteristic of any one in particular. Mystics have often indulged in methods of self-mortification, no doubt, but so too, and equally so, have non-mystics and anti-mystics. At the same time, there is something at the very heart and center of the mystical life which calls for and demands self-denial and severe discipline. Mystical experience, like the edelweiss, is something which flourishes at its best only on the Alpine uplands. It is not a product of the prairie corn belt or the flat, potato plain. There must be some stiff mountain-climbing, the spirit of adventure, a scorn of ease, and a defiance of peril. But the only forms of ascetic practice which are legitimate for a sound-minded mystic are forms that minister to self-discipline and that have to do with the athletic training of the soul for its daring adventures in the heights. As one climbs a great mountain, the paths which one can choose decrease in number as one approaches the top. There in the heights, divergent ways and by-paths disappear. At last, near the top, only *one* way is left, and that goes straight up toward the peak from which vast things can be seen.

All excellence is difficult. Mystical experience, by which I mean capacity to see the invisible, personal discovery of God, and joyous consciousness of divine presence, is no more difficult than any other supreme achievement. Holman Hunt once said to a lady who asked him how she could learn to make perfectly drawn, free-hand circles like his, that all she had to do was to practice eight hours a day for forty years! Then it would be as easy as breathing! Every great creator has something like that to say. When the years of toil and discipline are finished, the years of skill and triumph follow—the great creator acquires an unconscious skill:

> He builded better than he knew
> The conscious stones to beauty grew.
> The passive master lent his hand
> To the vast Soul that o'er him planned.

The mystic's asceticism, in so far as it is legitimate self-denial, is nothing more and nothing less than the "cost" of his way of life—the inherent price which must be paid for the "goods" upon which he has set his soul. It is involved in the very nature of self-conquest. The highest life is sure to call for all that a man hath. Nobody can help to build the Kingdom of God in the soul, and then in the world of men, without a stern elimination of all the unnecessary baggage which we mortals usually carry.

There have, of course, been so-called mystics in almost all centuries who have used ascetic methods to produce desirable states which they sought. They wanted to have visions and ecstasies and marvelous occurrences. They had discovered the psychological fact that long periods of abstinence—semi-starvation—bring an individual into a condition favorable to trance and ecstasy. So, too, do lacerations of the body and all assaults upon it which tend to produce temperature and fever. With the breaking-down of health, the weakening of vital forces, and of the tang and vigor of blood and muscle, suggestion operates more easily, and psychic concentration occurs almost without effort. The result is that when mystics, or pseudo-mystics as I should prefer to call them, have been eager for these phenomena, they have pushed mortification to an excess, and have welcomed that pitiful state of body which would let the soul have its swoons and raptures. This mistaken course naturally carries with it as severe risks as does drinking wood alcohol in order to get a moment of fullness of life.

The greater mystics have always seen that this is a false track. They have discounted visions and ecstasies. St. Teresa and St. John of the Cross spoke very sound and sensible words against all tendency to strain after morbid signs and supernatural marks of union with God, and they discounted every type of experience which did not add to the permanent moral and spiritual power of the life and character. Smaller mystics, who have given themselves periods of gruelling torture and long stretches of hunger to secure the spectacular results of the mystical way, have, in many cases, come to a deeper wisdom, and have given up, often at what seemed to them to be the command of God, all unnecessary austerities and all longing for these superficial signs of holiness.

The most terrible report of austerities with which I am familiar is that written by Henry Suso of his own self-imposed torments. The story found in his autobiography is a revolting one, too harrowing for repetition. One wonders how the poor man managed to live through the long years of his own ingenious cruelty and nightly agonies. Only a pathological patient could have planned, executed, and endured these methods of breaking down the natural man—"his comfort-seeking body"—as he puts it. But at length, that is, after more than twenty-five years, God showed him, by a series of visions, that he must cease these rigorous mutilations of himself and turn to a more normal and human way of life. The higher stage of his mystical experience came in that later, saner period of his life. He made at length the great discovery that "he who finds the inward in the outward is more spiritual than he who can only find the inward in the inward."

One of Suso's motives was his intense desire to feel and to imitate the sufferings of Christ. That desire has been a prolific source of sufferings with most mystics. They have taken very seriously the words of the Master: "He who would save his life must lose it," "He that would be my disciple must take up his cross," and they have followed with brave loyalty His way of "giving the all for the All." But it is a tendency which very easily becomes morbid and naturally ministers to a pathological condition. St. Francis of Assisi prayed at Alverna: "O Lord my Savior, I ask two favors before I die. Let me feel in my soul, in my body even, all the bitter pains which Thou hast felt. And in my heart, let me feel that immeasurable love which made Thee, Son of God, endure such sufferings for us poor sinners." Both prayers were answered in a remarkable measure. No one else perhaps has attained so nearly to the "immeasurable love" of Christ, and few certainly have felt more intensely than Francis did, the bitter pains which Christ bore. But Francis is at his highest and noblest when he is walking Christ's way of love and joy; not when, with agony of imitation, he is experiencing the stigmata of the nail prints.

All the mystics of the Middle Ages saw Christ in distorted perspective. They failed to see the happy, joyous, normal side of His life. The shadows of Gethsemane and Golgotha stretch back upon Him in their minds, and cover all his

years of life. The prophet's phrase, "a man
of sorrows," had become for them a character
description for Christ, which colored all the
gospel narratives. They could not believe that
His contemporaries ever thought of Him as a
happy diner at feasts, or as one who enjoyed
nature and social life, and felt at home with all
kinds and conditions of men and women. It
was over easy for anyone in the thirteenth or
fourteenth century to neglect the vivid details of
the gospels where these dealt with the human side
of the story, and to focus upon the supernatural
birth and the death and suffering which had won
their redemption. The obvious natural result of
this was that one who set out to imitate Christ
invariably felt that he must walk the hard path
of agony and crucifixion. The figure of the
suffering Christ was prominent in every church,
and it hung in the room of every person who
made religion the sum and substance of his life.
The constant thought of Christ as a sufferer, and
the readiness to follow Him in the way of the
Cross, tended, no doubt, to give depth and seri-
ousness to life; but it also tended to shift the
balance of life, to distort the perspective, to
glorify suffering as an end in itself, and to induce
the mystic expert to contrive artificial sufferings

rather than to go into the world of men, to take up and to share the burden of actual necessary human suffering.

I have now gone over many of the grounds for the extensive cult of suffering, and I have endeavored to explain why mystics have so often crucified their flesh. There is still, however, something more to say on the subject. The true mystic has, once for all, settled for himself the issues of life. He has ceased to "halt" between two aims. He has resolved to be a citizen of the spiritual kingdom—the city with foundations whose builder is God.

When a person has thus finally balanced his accounts and knows that all his important assets are in the spiritual world, it is natural to care intensely for that. To seek, to find, to love, and to be in union with God is his serious business. All rivalries are at an end. All secondary appeals become subordinate to the main concern. The ancient apostolic word is the mystic's battle-cry: "This one thing I do." The mystic, like St. Paul, is a "one-thinger" person. That means, as both William James and Evelyn Underhill tell us, that to be a genuine mystic one must form "new pathways of neural discharge." New habit tracks must be plowed. The wild jungle of the instincts

and passions must be organized. The old springs
of energy and action must be sublimated and
turned in new directions. The disordered life
must be brought into order. Its strife and jar
must be changed to peace and harmony. In short,
at whatever price, there must be a conquest of
the self. The old negation mystics call this process a "noughting of the self," self-annihilation.
"Nothing burneth in hell but self-will," says the
Theologia Germanica, "and therefore, it hath
been said, put off thine own will and there will
be no hell."

This only means, when translated into our
vocabulary, that we must stop seeking things
which are to belong to *one* and which cannot be
shared by all. As the same author elsewhere says,
we must learn to aim at "what is good without
any wherefore"; "He who is made a partaker of
the divine Nature neither willeth nor desireth nor
seeketh anything save Goodness as Goodness for
the sake of Goodness." John Woolman has
beautifully expressed this aim in that fine phrase
of his: "To turn all we possess into the channel
of universal love becomes the business of our
lives."

But that kind of conquest over the natural self
with its thrust of inborn instincts calls for a cam-

paign of warfare, in which nothing that belongs to the ease-loving, pleasure-loving, private ego is to be spared. Every Agag of that old nature is to be hewed in pieces before the Lord! That great expert in these matters, St. Thomas à Kempis, says: "If thou desirest to obtain victory, make ready for the battle. The crown of patience cannot be received where there has been no suffering. If thou wishest to be crowned, thou must fight manfully and suffer patiently; without labor none can obtain rest, and without contending there can be no conquest." What applies to the contest for the crown of patience is true of every spiritual crown, even the crown of life. Hegel's great words are forever true, and they apply here: "Die Tugend ist der höchste, vollendete Kampf."

No great religion, mystical or otherwise, is possible for us until we are cured of the subtle and persistent illusion of hedonism, until we are freed from the false, though very ancient, theory that we are beings created on purpose for the enjoyment of pleasure. William James, commenting on the view that men always act to get pleasure, very happily remarks: "As well might they suppose, because no steamer can go to sea without incidentally consuming coal, and because some steamers may occasionally go to sea to *try* their coal, that, therefore, no steamer *can* go to sea for any other motive than coal consumption."

The important mystics are men and women who have washed their souls clean of the hedonistic taint. They have a wholly different estimate of life. Pleasure, here or hereafter, is for them neither the aim nor the test of life. If one wants to see a man who has climbed clear above the pleasure line, and who lives in a height in which the pleasure spur is forgotten and has been left behind as though it did not exist, let him read St. John of the Cross. I admit that it sometimes seems to me as though, in leaving behind all reference to aspects of preference, of like and dislike, St. John of the Cross has also left behind our human way of life, and has withdrawn almost into a vacuum where exists very little of the air we mortals breathe. I feel the same way about Madame Guyon and Fenelon, who propose to themselves to attain to a state of absolute "indifference," in which they would pass beyond all consideration of the qualities of good and evil, of pleasure and pain, as inducements. Acts and situations cease to be considered in reference to those well-known coefficients. Every act is to be done solely for the love of God, not for any other reason whatsoever. I feel a sense of hush and awe in the presence of these tremendous lovers of God, but in my critical moments I am convinced that they are endeavoring to do what cannot be done, and, I am bound to add, what ought not to be done. They propose to eliminate all the springs of action which characterize us as men, to obliterate all the concrete clues from human experience which serve as practical guides for us, and to walk only by a supernatural pillar of cloud and fire from above.

Nevertheless, I verily believe that their way of life is sounder than the way of hedonism is. A pleasure theory sheds no light. It tells no one where to get on or where to get off. It gives no guidance on the problem of where we are going. It is dumb on all fundamental issues. It leaves one focused on a pure abstraction. It is like trying to kill a bear by aiming at him "all over." Pleasure? Yes, but what kind of pleasure, and attached to what aims and ends of life? If we are ever to get on with life-issues, we must neither be *indifferent*, nor must we talk that silly rubbish of aiming at pleasure—which means aiming at nothing in particular—as though one should say, "I am going to be a professional man, but I am never going to choose a *specific* profession! I am going to marry, but I am never going to fall in love with anyone in particular."

What the mystic means to say is, that he is out on a quest for "the shining table-lands to which our God himself is moon and sun," and having set his face to that business, no "toil of knees or heart or hands" terrifies him or turns him back. The man who sets out to climb unconquered mountains, or who proposes to fight his way over ice and through pitiless northern blizzards to the pole of the earth, trains for it, makes himself fit, and, absorbed as he is in an overmastering purpose, he forgets to consider what the butterfly and the dilettante call pleasure. It is not killed or annihilated; it is raised, sublimated, and fused in with the total purposes of the life. Pain is there too, but pain is forgotten. The agony of cold and hunger, the toil and weariness of climbing, the loneliness of days and nights, are merely an inherent part of the cost of this quest. So, too, with the mystic. He does not crucify himself, as though suffering were good in itself. He does not suppose that bludgeonings will win him merit. He is simply going a way of life which involves discipline, endurance, control. He becomes a spiritual athlete; he trains for his task. He pays the price for what seems to him a glorious venture. Pleasure goes out of his thought, because something much better and worthier of life comes in. Here is the testimony of St. Catherine of Sienna: "I would rather exert myself for Christ crucified, feeling pain, darkness and inner conflict, than not so exert myself and feel repose."

What all serious souls seek is a life with higher functions, not an escape from pain nor a primrose path to greater pleasures. John Stuart Mill in his rough phrase says just that: "I should rather be a man dissatisfied than a pig satisfied." It is better to enter into life halt and maimed, with eye blinded and right hand gone, than having a sound body to lose what we really mean by *life*. To have the hand with its cunning, the eye with its vast range of vision, the body free from pain, the gains of success, the pleasures that are believed to be most desirable, and yet to miss the interior dimension of life—what the young poet, C. H. Sorley, called "the inner and eternal Me"—and thus to be forever a starved shrunk soul, is to confuse all sense of values. Rossetti's sonnet, "Lost Days," paints this tragedy for us:

> I do not see them here; but after death
> God knows I know what faces I shall see,
> Each one a murdered self, with low, last breath.

"I am thyself,—what hast thou done to me"?
"And I—and I—thyself (lo! each one saith),
And thou thyself to all eternity!"

The mystic is a person who has succeeded in attaining what Christ called "a single eye." Most of us would love the highest if we saw it, but we see so many interesting things and are drawn hither and thither by their attractions, that we often miss the one thing that matters. It is a solemn fact that our dominant desire is what settles our destiny. William James humorously tells of a man who had one chance to visit Europe and see its rare and wonderful treasures, but after his return his one topic of conversation was about the window-fastenings in the hotels where he stayed! That was his central interest. The mystic has found the one thing that absorbs his soul; it is God, and with his eye focused on that end, he refuses to be swerved from his quest by the multitudinous appeals of side issues. The *Theologia Germanica* says that man was created with an eye for perceiving time and created things, and with another eye for seeing into eternity, but that one of these eyes must close if the other is to see its object. That view, which is often taken to be the essential view of mysticism, makes the holder of it very stern toward the outer world. It forces him to say to every visible thing,

Stand thou on that side, for on this am I.

I believe, however, that the soundest modern mystics do not draw the dividing line quite at that cleavage. The spiritual must not be set over against the visible and tangible, or the eternal over against the temporal, as though they were two sundered and individual worlds. What we need to acquire is the seeing eye that sees through the visible and temporal, in clairvoyant fashion, and discovers the eternal and the spiritual here and now revealed in the midst of time and things. My sympathies still go out to a little boy of whom I used to hear many years ago. He was busy making mud pies when a kind lady came by and said, "Come with me and I will wash you up and tell you how you can get to be a beautiful angel up in heaven." He protested, "I don't want to be an angel up in heaven; I want to be an angel down here in the dirt!" Our real concern, I am sure, ought to be not to find a spiritual realm of calm and joy divorced from this checkerboard world of black and white, but to find and to hold firmly to the eternal and spiritual values, revealed here in the strange mixture of light and dark which we call *life*. And this, once more, is a matter of *seeing*—not a question of spectacles or far-sight lenses, but a question of a *seeing eye*.

It is a well-known principle of psychology that perception is always accomplished through a stock of apperceiving material in the beholder's mind. He perceives the new object or event through the mass of memories and associations which operates within him unconsciously, and through which the new experience is interpreted with meaning. It is literally true that we perceive only what we *apperceive*—only what we can interpret in terms of earlier experience. If we lost our stock of accumulations from experience, we should thereby lose our world.

This same principle applies, too, to the world within, the world of spiritual realities. We cannot see it, we cannot find it, if we have no stock of life with which to view it and to interpret it. We must, in some sense, preperceive it, apperceive it, have some sure clue to what we are seeking, or we gaze blankly at nothing and come at length to accept the ancient materialist conclusion that only the ponderable is real. This principle means, then, that the severity which we are to practice with ourselves is not to be found in starving "brother ass," the body, nor in a flight from the world of tasks and turmoil, but it is to be found in an unceasing discipline of the soul's capacity of vision. This achievement of seeing through the husks and veils of the finite, and of finding here, in the midst of time and sense, the Life and Love of God is surely not simpler or easier than is the attainment of perfect taste, or of perfect courtesy of manners, or of the highest creative skill in art or music, or of that sure wisdom and power that enable a statesman like Lincoln to see his way in the maze and jungle of temporal problems. It comes and can come only through the slow accumulation of insight and depth, the practice of discrimination as fine as that which gives poise and balance to the tight-rope walker, the discipline of silence and hush, the urge of a spirit that will not stop its quest until the tiny rill has channeled and canyoned its way to the ocean from which it sprang. But the stern way of life entails no hatred of life. It is not world-flight. It is not a way of defiance and irrationality. It does not rail at the beauty of this outer world or call human love common and unclean. It only insists that the finite is never a terminus; it is meant to be a thoroughfare on into the Heart and Life of God.

Life has no other logic
And time no other creed
Than: I for joy will follow
Where thou for love dost lead.

CHAPTER III

MYSTICISM AND RELIGIOUS EDUCATION

IF mysticism is to make any vital appeal to our generation it must be interpreted in current terms of thought, not in the forms of thought that dominated the third century or the fourteenth. It perhaps may be said that an experience is forever just an *experience*, and that what we seek is an accurate report of what the experience is in its own inner nature, not an interpretation of it. But as a plain matter of fact we have no experiences, not even our most simple sense experiences, which we do not interpret. It is only a question of degree. Sometimes we keep closer to the bare *feel* of what is "given" and at other times we more obviously translate the "given" fact in terms and colors of our accumulated mass of past experiences. But nothing ever enters and passes through our minds without being reborn and transformed by the passage. A "pure sensation" is an artificial construction of the psychologist, not something that is ever actually experienced.

In the same way, if one is really to find God the discovery of Him must *mean* something and not remain a bare, abstract, though glorified, *Blank*.

The great classical mystics have, no doubt, made very much of the attainment of a state in which the particular and concrete vanish and fall away, and the soul seems to be ushered into contact with the universal One and All. Many writers have consequently insisted that no experience is rightly called "mystical" unless the recipient of it has passed beyond all finite and specific qualities and characteristics, and stands in a hushed and trembling contact with an All that is at the same time Nothing. My answer would be that these classical mystics were tied to a system of metaphysics which assumed that the infinite and absolute Reality, which for them was God, must be above and beyond all that is finite and so imperfect, and in their quest for God they were constrained to climb into the thin air of the pure abstract universal.

In deinem Nichts hoff Ich das All zu finden.

For us today, at least for me, the abstract universal is only a cheap infinite and no solution of any of our deepest issues of life. A mysticism that ended on the barren apex of the abstract One would leave me cold, though I feel deep respect for all it meant to the spiritual heroes of the past who have climbed the lonely peak of this mystical Mount Everest.

The God of our quest is more than a vague Beyond, more than a bare ultimate Reality. He is a God with concrete character. He is revealed wherever higher and more ideal forms of life are conquering and supplanting the lower ones. Wherever the shining tents of the forces of light are pitched against the armies of darkness, there God is creating His new world. He is the God of beauty and truth. He lives and expresses Himself through the spirit of love and self-giving. Where love is, God is; and, therefore, where love is incarnated at its best there God is most nearly incarnated. Where the curve of human life rises highest above the low and mean and cruel, and nearest to the ideal of unselfish goodness, there God is most clearly to be found. God is never characterless and abstract. He is infinitely rich in the concrete. He is Spirit, not abstract Being, and Spirit is essentially self-revealing—the Life that pours itself through history and art and religion. There are many persons who possess a capacity for the discovery of God—a certain sensitiveness of contact with this realm of the Spirit beyond the frontiers of the seen and the tangible. It may well be that these spiritual experts have a real contribution to make, and that they will extend the borders of our universe, as the musicians and creative artists have done.

It would indeed be strange if men had inherent capacities which functioned fruitlessly in a vacuum, if there were tentacles of the soul which never prehended anything real. It would be pitiful if we were made for the enjoyment of a world which we could never, even dimly, sight or hail; if there were never any *answer* to all this palpitation of ours for the Beyond. The capacity must surely be either a functionless survival of a *power of correspondence* that worked successfully once in some remote ancestor of ours—some happy Adam in an unspoiled Eden—or it is a dawning prophecy of powers of correspondence which will somewhere, some day, come full into play, as our eye, originally sprung from a protoplasmic sensitive spot on the skin that was, at first, merely *aware* of a near-presence, now detects the substances that are actually burning on the surface of Sirius or Aldebaran. Anyway there are persons who are convinced that the correspondence is not one-sided, that *something answers back*.

Our external world, as we now know, is full of realities for which we have no adequate end-organs of perception. We have no "eyes" to see molecules, atoms, electrons, microbes, X-rays, radio-vibrations, or multitudes of other physical phenomena, which are as certainly *there* as are the Matterhorn or Mt. Katahdin. We have succeeded in proving the existence of these non-perceptible realities by other methods than unaided senses. We now know that our world out there is vastly richer than the reports of our senses would have led us to suspect. This demonstration is the slow result of ages of coördinated observation, experiment, invention, formulation, and verification. It has at last put at our hand a world of which no ancient or medieval philosopher dreamed, and it gives us ground for expecting an almost limitless expansion of this world of actual, but invisible, realities and energies.

The mystics, I shall conclude are those highly sensitized persons whose lives seem to lie open inwardly to the presence of an immanent Life and who bear witness to a deeper universe of Spirit, undergirding and penetrating all that is seen and touched. We have no specific "senses" for this experience. We cannot demonstrate the existence of the Spirit as we can the fact of a mountain or a planet. We have not learned how to coördinate and verify the experiences of our spiritual geniuses—the seers and prophets and poets—so that the mystic side of life is left inarticulate, vague, fleeting, unfruitful, and for some persons dubious and suspect. Nevertheless there is an accumulation of testimony that is august and weighty. The mystic himself is so overwhelmingly convinced that he has burst into a world beyond the frontiers of sense that he cares very little for proof and demonstration, and he seldom does much to show how bridges can be built across for common, everyday wayfarers to travel over.

There has been a persistent tendency to confuse genuine mystical experience with occult phenomena. This has happened in all ages as it is happening now, and quite naturally so; for the line between the mystical and the occult is notoriously hard to draw or define. Automatisms, communication with disincarnate spirits, the perception of auras, telepathy and telaesthesia, are forms of psychic phenomena which are receiving searching study and investigation, and they will eventually be given their true valuation. Many of these phenomena are the result, not of fraud or malicious deception, but of peculiar traits of psychic disposition which have only recently received the attention of scientific research. We shall know some day whether they are the fruit of sheer abnormality, or whether they are indications of "gifts" which may have, at least in some cases, constructive and revealing value.

Genuine mystical experience, on the other hand, that is, the type that enriches the religious life of men and brings creative energies for the spiritual tasks of the race, is a very different matter. It is due primarily, certainly with the pillar mystics, to some added range and scope of native mental capacity rather than to abnormalities of nerves. It promotes health and sanity. It heightens moral power. It vastly increases one's ability to stand the universe. It brings into play immense energies for reorganizing and rebuilding the moral and spiritual world, and it has thus, if not a survival value in the narrow sense, at least a sustaining and conquering value.

With this brief survey of the nature of mystical experience, I turn to consider methods of education which may promote the nobler aspects of such experience. There are two characteristically different types of education. One of them puts the emphasis on information; the other puts the main emphasis on the formation of life and character. The two types cannot of course be sharply divided asunder, but the aim and focus in the one case will be quite unlike the aim and focus in the other. Our educational systems for the last hundred years have been primarily concerned with information, instruction in reference to objective facts, and with practical results. They have been keyed to produce persons who could find the resources of nature and who could *do* the things that needed to be done in our world. This educational policy has been subtly and unconsciously preparing the way for the theory that man's specific "behavior" is the matter of real importance about him. His interior life is more or less negligible and may be shelved without·being seriously missed. The emphasis in education has been acutely, even thumpingly, objective and scientific. The laboratories have been busy with the conquest and control of the external world. They have cashed in immense results. Every form and type of exact research have been quickened and perfected. The atom has opened up its mysteries in this century as the solar system did in the seventeenth. We have counted forty thousand gigantic suns in the space occupied by what the ancient world believed to be "the seven stars" of the Pleiades. We have cut down through the mounds which mark the sites of Ur and Babylon, Jericho and Megiddo, and we now know not only what kind of pottery they used in the different stages of their development, but we know also in pretty full detail the characteristics of their civilization back to the dawn of their organized social life.

Not satisfied with interlacing the entire world with cables and wires and electric communication, we have now learned how to vibrate our music and our words across wireless spaces, through mountains and oceans, so that soon the entire population of the United States can hear the President read his inaugural address, and a single teacher can give language lessons to everybody in Europe from one broadcasting station. No oil is too deep or too remote to elude us. We ransack the poles for economic resources. We say to mountains, if they are in our way, "Be removed and be cast into the sea." We have refined the methods of warfare until guns and cannon seem as crude as Maori spears or Zulu arrows. We can kill now with poisons which leave no wounds and perhaps in time they will leave no mourners! The emphasis, I say, has been on methods of education that would promote the conquest and control of external nature and that would prepare persons who could *do* things successfully. There is no question about the results. The methods have *worked.* We can fly. We can travel at enormous speed. We can talk around the world. We can see what is happening on the surface of the sun and we are near neighbors with the Pharaohs of Moses' time.

But unfortunately this conquest of the external world does not make us better men. Our "I. Q." is high, but our hearts are neither trained nor spiritualized. We know a great deal about radium and helium but we know very little about the deeper processes of the Soul. We are not any more "at home" with our universe than in the ages when men's sight was more limited and their voices carried less far. Our losses and agonies and perplexities are just as baffling and as hard to bear as when speeds were confined to ten miles an hour. It is not much comfort to a man to know that he could buy the whole of Palestine as it was in Christ's day and not feel the outlay much more than he feels paying his income tax, if with this accumulation of goods he is missing all of the peace and joy of life which Christ promised men. We quite obviously need to bring up the neglected side of life and to consider more seriously than we have done a type of education which will enable us to find *ourselves* and to recover interior peace and joy and power.

I shall admit at once that I have no ready-made technique to propose for this new education. I shall not solve the problem by laying down here a magic method by which we can all become saints and prophets. If I knew such a formula I would not propose it. I am suspicious of short-cut and "labor-saving" schemes, which promise to give us millenniums by "limited express"—what the French happily call, "grande vitesse." It is the business not of one man but of the combined educational forces, coöperating through years of experience and experiment, to give us a successful technique for our *new* education. It is merely my humble purpose now to drive home the fact that our present education is one-sided, inadequate, and pitiably neglectful of the inner life—the making of persons—and to indicate the lines along which the new education should move, if it is to correct the false emphasis.

First of all we must push education, and all that we mean by spiritual culture, very much farther back toward the headwaters of the child's life. Very often the child's chance for a genuinely religious life has been lost before what we usually call his "education" has begun. Many of our native capacities are transitory; they fade away and become atrophied and functionless if they are "starved" at the period when they "ripen" and call for stimulus and activity. Fortunately the religious capacity is not as short-lived in most of us as are many of our instincts, but it is nevertheless true that the impulse and urge to correspond with the unseen and the beyond appear very early in life, and they are profoundly, though of course unconsciously, affected by suggestion and by the social atmosphere of the family and the child's group life. Religion in its primary stage is not a body of ideas that have been systematically taught, but rather an attitude of life, a tendency of the will, a spring of faith, which have been formed through unconscious imitation and contagion. No child ever knows how he comes to have confidence in the external world, but his faith in it is largely due to the unquestioning faith that everybody else has in it. So, too, if God is real to those who form the child's social group, He quickly becomes an essential part of the child's life.

What we vaguely call "temperament" and "disposition" are much more important matters for an individual's life than are houses or lands or bank accounts. There is no doubt a hereditary factor which plays a part in shaping these subtle inner aspects of character, but they are in large degree determined by the social environment in which the early formative years are passed. The methods of discipline which meet the child's moods and acts; the personal quality of the lives of those who deal most closely with him; surrounding influences of beauty and love, or the lack of them; the presence, or the absence, of nervous frictions and irritations and fears; sympathetic and understanding appreciation of what is going on in the developing mind and heart; in a word, the atmosphere, the invisible spirit, of the home —these are the great forces which form the disposition and temperament of the child. If we were anything like as much concerned to discover these methods and processes, and the technique of this creative business, as we are to discover the laws of chemical composition, we should soon have a valuable body of principles for the guidance of those who are the moral and spiritual guardians of little children. We know how to control electrical energies but we have not learned how to shape and control the formation of disposition.

The foremost religious races, notably the Hebrews and the Greeks, were great adepts in the cultivation of the imagination of their children.

Imagination is a mental capacity of the first importance for every aspect of life, but peculiarly so for religion. The power to *see*, to forecast, to anticipate, to discover, and to value what is implicated or involved in the normal experiences of life is an essential spiritual capacity. It is what the New Testament means by *faith*, what George Santayana calls "the soul's invincible surmise." It is fully as important as that power to apprehend and describe *facts*, which we have learned how to train with such success. But matter of fact people as we incline to be, we are apt to be afraid of imagination. We assume that it has to do with "what isn't there," with the world of illusion and hallucination, with exaggeration and untruth. It is, however, a gift of major rank—this faculty of vision, this capacity to feel realities which elude the senses, but which are there for *seeing* souls and for those who have "the single eye." It is as necessary for religion as the power to see perspective is for drawing, and it is no more difficult to cultivate than is the latter. But we have not done it, and we do not do it. We train children to see and to dodge passing automobiles, a skill which is essential to survival, but we neglect the cultivation of the capacity *to see the invisible*, which is essential to art, to poetry, and to religion. I am advocating no slackening of attention to the automobile, but only more attention to the subtler realities which form and build the dimensions of the soul.

Meditation is well-nigh a lost art in our Western civilization. It is, however, extremely important for the cultivation of interior depth and insight and moral power. Suggestion and expectation are mighty agencies in the formation of character. The heightening power that comes through concentration is one of the most important contributions that education ever makes. It is comparable to the addition of a new psychic capacity. Count Keyserling is certainly right when he says that "culture, in its real sense, is not to be achieved by way of widening the surface, but by a change of plane in terms of depth, and this growing more profound depends upon the degree of concentration."[1] The awakening of wonder and admiration is at least as significant for the growth of the soul as the birth of question-asking is. Mothers in India begin to train their children in silent meditation long before they are taught letters or counting. An education that does nothing to cultivate and fertilize the deep subsoil of the child's life is to say the least weak

[1] *Travel Diary*, Vol. I, p. 273.

and superficial. Movies and jazz are poor substitutes for the inward discipline of hush and
quiet. One of the greatest debts I owe my family
for my early religious culture is due to the custom
of silent worship every morning after breakfast.
It was a busy home with heavy burdens of duties
and labors, but we allowed nothing to interfere
with the hush of worship which fed our lives with
vital energies for the tasks of the day. The habit
of turning the mind from outward things and
events to an attitude of love and confidence toward an invisible presence became as natural to
me as breathing. Children are far more mystical-
minded than their elders suspect, and mystics
would not be so rare if we made better use of the
culture of silence in the lives of our children.

One of the most important features of early
education is the organization of instincts and emotions in the formation of loyalties. Most of our
coarser primitive instincts, such as fear, hate,
anger, and the springs of action which concern
the ego, are stronger than are actually needed for
survival and for development in the environment
which "civilization" furnishes. These instincts
are not "wicked." They are not tainted with
"original sin." They are the raw material which
is to be reshaped and molded into character.

They must not of course be eliminated, but they need to be refined and "sublimated." This is best done by taking them up and fusing them into wider "systems of interest," which include others besides the egoistic self. "Play" concerns more than one. It involves some sort of common rules, habits, and ends to be accomplished. No one can learn to "play" without coördinating with others, without give and take, without some degree of submission, or without forecasting purposes which draw upon instinct, emotion, interest, imagination, and ingenuity. From "play" it is possible to pass to ever higher and wider *unities of purpose*, which will organize more springs of action around a central aim and so develop a loyalty system. Loyalties through which the individual becomes dedicated to aims and causes that unite many persons toward a common goal of life are among the highest formative forces known to us. Loyalty to mother and to father and to family, loyalty to the play group, to the school group, the church group, are good foundations for the more abstract loyalties which build our lives, such as loyalty to truth, to duty, to honor, loyalty to ideals and to our Great Companion. Here are the sources of power that underlie our morality, our faith, and our religion, and all that constitutes rich personal character. These things are all built on loyalities, and the formation of such loyalties is thus at least as important an achievement as is learning the multiplication table or becoming skilled in the right use of pronouns.

Instincts have for centuries been cited as the conservative forces which entail the ancient, age-long habits and the primitive traits of the race. Again and again, it is said, "What has been is what shall be," and "What has been done is what shall be done," because we are creatures of instincts and emotions and these are endlessly repeatable forces, i.e., the same in all generations. Yes, but instincts and emotions need not remain forever blind, impulsive, and explosive driving-engines. Once gasoline was a highly dangerous explosive. We have learned to make it explode in such minute quantities and so rapidly that it drives our car forward and does not blow it up in one shattering catastrophe. It is just the business of education to bring higher motives into mastery over lower impulses, and out of chaotic "urges" to organize an intelligent and coöperative person whose life culminates in that overarching loyalty—loyalty to the unseen Person who is the indwelling Life of our lives.

One of the most important influences in the

formative culture of the soul is the right use of great spiritual literature, especially of course the Bible. It is the best means within our reach for the cultivation of imagination. It spontaneously kindles loyalty to what is true and fine and noble, and it helps more powerfully than any other influence I know of to foster the experience of unseen things. But we use these means bunglingly, awkwardly, and ineffectively. There are few more tragic blunders in the history of spiritual education than the modern Sunday School presents. It is not as effective for its purpose as the ancient Hebrew Synagogue was, or as the early Christian Catechetical School. There are, no doubt, Sunday Schools which are centers of great spiritual culture and there are single classes in many other Sunday Schools where the children find their way across the frontiers of the everyday life into a world of spiritual beauty and joy and consecration. But alas, much of our Sunday School teaching is dull, uninspiring, and unpedagogical. It does not impart a knowledge of the Great Book of the ages nor does it arouse a lasting love for it, or faith in its truths.

The trouble frequently is that an attempt is made to force upon the mind of the youth a certain theory of Scripture, though more often the constructive effect of the teaching is blocked by an effort to lug in a "moral" at every point, or to drive home a religious lesson from every narrative. The total effect is artificial and unnatural. The more or less recalcitrant youth do not analyze the situation. They cannot give a clear account of what is wrong with their Sunday School, but they dimly know that something is the matter with it and that they go with lagging feet and with a lack of interest. In many cases a positive dislike of the Bible is produced, while in a multitude of cases nothing which can properly be called spiritual culture is accomplished. Something similar happens in preparatory schools with the great "classics" which are required for college entrance. I find that many young persons abominate the "classics" on which they entered college. The trouble is that the *fact* elements are minutely stressed, but the imaginative quality is missed and so the joy in the creative work is lost.

If chemistry and physics were studied in the same rambling, hit-or-miss fashion which we apply to our study of Scripture we should never have discovered the truth about atoms or electricity. There is a vast amount of illuminating historical material at hand to interpret the background of the Old and the New Testament books. It is possible now to know the dramatic and vital issues which are woven into the tissues of this marvelous literature of the Spirit. There is hardly a line in these books which does not have a deep human interest and appeal, but almost nothing of all this filters down to the teacher of our boys and girls. The dramatic and vital aspects are masked and hidden. The thrilling heroic narrative is spoiled to make place for a pious "lesson." The teacher is not an expert in kindling imagination, in imparting vision, in making the unseen real, in fascinating the hearer with the story of national struggle, personal heroism, and undying loyalty. I know the difficulties of securing such expert teachers, particularly in rural communities, and I know that I am calling for gifts that are none too common, but my main point is this: We have not waked up to the ominous fact that the Sunday School has gone awry, and that the immense opportunity of drawing the children and youth of our land into the higher spiritual life and into possession of an enlarged inner life and vision is being, if not lost, then certainly bungled and misused. It ought to be a school of prophets, a place for the true culture of the soul, where the springs of the will would be raised to new power, the faith and loyalty of the heart elevated, and the vision of the soul quickened for correspondence with the vast spiritual environment in which we live, or at least should live!

Few things in our present-day civilization are so extraordinary as the increase in the number of young men and women who secure a college or university education. No one who has the mental capacity for what we call "advanced education" need miss it. There is an institution of higher learning within reach of every community, and poverty is no longer a bar to such learning. An immense group of men and women go forth with their degrees each year into the life of the nation, and should of course be raising the entire intellectual and moral level of the population. But we get frequent suggestive intimations that the effect is not all that we have reason to expect, while occasionally we have rude awakenings to the fact that much of our so-called "higher culture" is crude and unspiritual. One has only to spend very little time in almost any college or university center to see why this is so. In most cases the institutions have grown in size beyond their capacity to assimilate and to organize the raw material which pours in as to an immense knowledge factory. The human contacts between professors and students are slight. Truth is imparted too much in wholesale fashion, as one turns on a hose. Some receive the full gush and some only the thin spray. Student bodies are inclined to be great psychological masses, powerfully under the influence of group suggestion and subject in high degree to imitation and contagion, and they live in a dizzy whirl of activities, athletics, fraternities, social festivities, and extraneous aims. A good amount of honest work is done, and all our institutions graduate some excellent scholars and train some noble characters, but everywhere the emphasis is wrong and the educational waste is pitiful. In our rush for big institutions, big endowments, big numbers, big athletic victories, we have almost forgotten that the business of a college is to make moral and spiritual *persons*. We have laboratories for everything but that. The forces that should shape and mold the inner life of our students are meager and feeble. Everything here is capricious and accidental. The chapel is an antiquated spiritual weapon and the college Y.M.C.A. is too often an amorphous affair.

Moral and spiritual influences must be fundamental, inherent, and integral in the fiber and fabric of the college life. If the classes in biology, history, psychology, and philosophy disintegrate the faith of the student, it cannot be re-covered and reintegrated by a spray of rosewater at chapel. The moral and spiritual life is not something apart, to be superadded to life as a kind of perfume. It must spring out of and be a vital part of the normal life and thought of the individual. The professor who teaches biology or psychology is the person who for better or worse is to give the student his spiritual bearings in that field, and the influences of the classroom will make him either see, or fail to see, the religious implications of the truth he is learning. We should not wish to shackle any man's mind, or to force truth to fit into any traditional molds, but we should insist that those who train our sons and daughters shall be *reverent interpreters of truth*, persons who feel a genuine concern for the moral and spiritual *effect* of their work upon the making of the lives which pass under their hands.

Here, again, I am simply pleading that we should wake up to the patent fact that our higher institutions of learning are weak precisely where they ought to be strong. We have built marvelous dormitories, observatories, laboratories, chapels, gymnasiums, and stadiums. We have endowed professorial chairs and provided for perpetual fellowships, but we have spent very little money and much less thought on the central problem, how to build the interior lives of our students and how, out of the crude, raw material, to train and develop persons who have depth of insight, clear vision, and spiritual perception of the meaning of life; profound loyalties, broad comprehension, magnanimous aims, and withal an appreciation of those subtle energies of the Spirit revealed within the soul.

The minister of today, whether in a city church or in a rural community, has a very wide sphere of duties and functions. He must touch many sides of the life of his complex flock and he must be the leader in a great array of activities. He is much more than a "voice" crying from a pulpit. He should have organizing capacity, undoubted qualities of leadership, a grasp of social and economic problems with sense enough not to have his sermons deal primarily with these topics, some real insight into the bearing of science and history on the central realities of religion, and of course a deep and intimate knowledge of Scripture and Christian literature. But with all his "gettings," he must above everything else get a vital, first-hand acquaintance and fellowship with God. His messages must spring out of experience and be touched and fused with some real inner contact with the spiritual realm from which the soul is nourished. Seminaries where ministers are trained should, therefore, be nurseries of mystical life and experience. Our theology should spring out of tested and verified experience—the experience of the individual and the race. It should be constantly reëxamined and revised, as all truth in this unfolding world should be. We must not be enthusiastic disciples of Lot's wife, looking backward fondly on the systems of thought which the past has constructed. The primary emphasis should be upon training persons of deep religious life and first-hand experience, with all-round spiritual leadership. Traditional theology should give place to sound psychological and philosophical interpretation of man's true inner nature as it really is. The unveiling of God and the revelation of man which Christ brought to light have been strangely neglected for substitute views which have a dubious pagan origin. The Galilean way of life and the truly Christian conception of God and man should be freshly presented to every person who is to be a spiritual guide in our modern world.

But besides all this, every seminary should have one or more experts in the mystical way of life. The cultivation of the inner life must not be left to chance and accident. In using the word "expert," I mean a person who "has been there," who not only knows the literature of this field but who has seriously traveled this way of life. There should be some real experiments made in the use of silence and meditation, and there should be an illuminating course in the writings and interpretations of the great mystics. Technical, historical knowledge is not enough; there is need of sympathetic, appreciative interpretation with, as I have said, some well-guided attempts to practice the presence of God. In all such matters personal leadership counts for most and disciples will be pretty sure to arrive if the master himself knows and travels the way on in front.

I am not concerned to propose any technique or to outline any specific course for seminary students. My purpose here is merely to insist upon a new emphasis. I want to see a harvest of ministers produced who not only know the Bible and the history of the Church, but who know God as well, who have a warm human touch with men and at the same time are in immediate correspondence with the world within the world we see. I should like to appeal strongly for a deeper psychology of man's inner life and for a new flood of light upon the relation of the human and the divine, the finite spirit, and the environing infinite Spirit. We have spent much precious time with the husks and the fringes of spiritual truth; now the hour has struck for us to focus upon the center and refresh ourselves with a knowledge of the innermost realities by which we live.

What power would mark the preacher's words if he could say with Isaac Penington: "This is He, this is He: there is no other. This is He whom I have waited for and sought after from my childhood. I have met with my God. I have met with my Saviour. I have felt the healings drop upon my soul from under His wings."

CHAPTER IV

THE BEARING OF MYSTICAL EXPERIENCE ON
ORGANIZATION AND SYSTEM

SOME person of humor and insight has said:
"Christ promised that where two or three are
gathered together anywhere in the world in His
name He will meet with them, but now in our
present world wherever three are met together a
proposal is immediately made to form an organization, and one of the three persons will be chairman, one will be secretary, and the third one
treasurer!" This is not just humor; it corre-
sponds somewhat fairly to a real difference between primitive Christianity and modern efficiency. We want to get things done; we aim at
results. Christ, on the other hand, was concerned
to have men's lives flooded with the consciousness
of God, to have them become "rich in God." He
is always assisting men to "enter into life." But
are the two diverse aims inconsistent and exclusive? Is it not possible to have both aims united
in a larger synthesis? May we not become effi-

cient in fact just because we have succeeded in finding God? Can we not be flooded with the consciousness of God and at the same time perfect some form of organization that will be the effective body and instrument of that experience? That is the goal of this search.

If we should take Christ's message and way of life as our standard of Christianity, if we should set it up as our criterion of "orthodoxy," and call all deviation from it "heresy," then I suppose we should find "heresy" prevailing almost everywhere in all periods of Church history, and we should gather here and there from the vast prairie harvest of the ages only a few fragrant flowers of "orthodoxy." The "heresy-hunters," however, so far as I know, have never made that model their mark and badge of the true faith. They have always had another measuring rod in their mind when they have essayed to measure the faith of a man, though St. Paul stoutly asserts that "he who does not possess the spirit of Christ is none of His."

The Church quickly though no doubt unconsciously, left behind the Galilean type of religion —the religion of life—and introduced another type more consonant with the intellectual climate of the Greco-Roman world. This shift of level was bound to take place under the conditions of life and thought that existed then, and we do not need to spend any time weeping over the course which historical movements have taken, any more than we should weep over the bends and curves of the Kennebec or the Mississippi in their on-ward sweep. It was better to have the Christian movement take the line of transformation which it did take, to swing out and in this way make con-quest of the Aegean cities and the Italian penin-sula, than it would have been to have it remain locked up in Syrian Palestine, a religion touching only a small fraction of a single race, with no more outlet than the Dead Sea has. If it was to circulate, it was sure to adjust to the forms of thought, imagination, and emotion which filled the minds of men where the track of its currents lay.

But while we do not spend our time weeping over the strange circuits of history, we may at least endeavor to understand what has actually happened. What we find when we go back to the birth of our religion is that it began as a *way of life*. It was in the first instance an experience of God. It was saturated with the consciousness of God. We are confronted in the earliest stage of Christianity with a new type of Person, a new creation. We have so persistently asked, after the Hellenic manner, what did Christ *teach*, what were His ideas, what concepts did He hold and communicate? that we are always in danger of forgetting what manner of Person He was, how He felt, and what He loved and what He *was*. First and foremost His life should concern us— His experience should interest us. We have had books enough on the ethics of Jesus, the economics of Jesus, the sociology of Jesus. We need a book on the experience of Jesus. It is always there behind His words, flooding through them, inundating all He says with a tone and power that are unique and incomparable. Everything is Alpine and comes out of heights. He always *is* what He says and what He does. He is vastly more than "Q" reports. He is what He awakens in others. He is what He has been creatively doing for men and with men through these intervening centuries. There is no use trying to interpret Him until the interpreter can rise above dry, wooden concepts and can feel first-hand the marvelous depth and height, the infinite inward grandeur, of His personal life and experience.

We argue endlessly in the Rabbinical manner about His theory of the Kingdom of God. As soon as we begin to use the eyes of our heart, we see that whatever else it may be, the Kingdom of God is the kind of life He was living here among men. It is a new experience of God as Father— not a new theory of the Fatherhood of God. They are totally different things. It is a new experience of the organizing, transforming, and constructive power of love in the relations of life between man and man—not a new *theory* of brotherhood, not a new sociology, not a new ethics. It is a strange and wonderful consciousness of new and untried spiritual forces. He feels them surging through His life first and He sets them circulating through other lives wherever He finds in men an answering and responsive faith. Much more important than what He thought about the fall of Jerusalem, or about the apocalyptic theories of his age, or about His own Messianic mission, was His own discovery of the love and grace of God, and that this love and grace flowed like an inexhaustible fountain through Him. He Himself is the revelation of the Kingdom. The reign of God was actually in operation there in that life. We see at last what love can do. Spear and cross cannot defeat it. We know now that there are no mountains that can hold out against faith like that. This is the spirit that overcomes the world and inaugurates a kingdom which triumphs over all material empires, for it has done it.

Dr. A. C. McGiffert, for whose work I have unbounded respect and admiration, tells us that Jesus had no new ideas of God. "His idea of God was wholly Jewish. At no point, so far as we can judge from the synoptic Gospels, did He go beyond His peoples' thought of God."[1] Nevertheless the story of the Prodigal Son is saturated with an insight, an emotional tone, and an attitude of heart that are found nowhere else in religious literature. It could probably be shown by the same kind of rigid historical analysis which Dr. McGiffert uses that Beethoven had no new ideas of symphony and that Raphael had no new ideas of madonnas. That analytical historical method misses the main point. If one goes back over the stages of history or of biology with certain reigning categories in his mind, it is difficult to discover where anything "new" has emerged. The new appears to be only the old come back with a slight increment or with a tiny change of setting and context. But when one shakes himself free from his inadequate categories and learns to estimate values and shifts of level with the vision of an awakened and crea-

[1] *The God of the Early Christians*, p. 21.

tive mind, then it is seen that the appearance of the new, the unique, the novel is by no means a rare event which seems miraculously to break in upon and interrupt the unvarying recurrence of the past. The old "stuff" may still be there but reorganized, sublimated, raised to a new level, gifted with new capacities, or shot through with new powers, so that a watershed is crossed, an epoch begun.

A molecule is composed of old atoms, but how different from the atoms before organization raised them to their new order. H_2O is absolutely unlike H and O. Life is old matter organized in new and unpredictable ways. The ideas that come and go before the footlights of consciousness are seldom new-born ideas. They are "new" because they take on new meaning in the quickening life of a new-born experience. They emerge out of the alchemy of experience remade, transformed, new-molded, even though they may still be current with old names. Christ had a new *experience of God*. He let the Life and Love of God break through Him. You could feel the Heart of God palpitating there in Him as it had done nowhere else so adequately. God meant to Him what He had never meant to anybody else, and He raised that meaning to its supreme height in others, as Beethoven made symphony mean more than it ever meant before and Raphael made motherhood mean something infinitely wonderful.

I feel that here is where my friend Professor Kirsopp Lake falls short. His *Hibbert Journal* article on Jesus shows impressively all the limitations of the scientific method when it is applied to personality and to spiritual values.[2] You cannot deal with a human heart exactly as you deal with a triangle or a parallelopipedon. Categories which work admirably for describable facts fall short and break down utterly when they are used to interpret the unique creations of genius or when they undertake to assess a life which reveals the eternal in the midst of time. Long enough we have tried by methods of reduction to explain the higher in terms of the lower. We have leveled down the novel "mutation," because we have insisted that it could not be thought of as higher than "its source and origin." Now we are coming to see that this is a universe in which forms and realities *emerge* that were not here before, and that cannot be assessed or explained in terms of what was here before. They are what they

[2] The article on Jesus was reprinted in Lake's *Religion Yesterday and Tomorrow.*

do, what they lead on to, not what they came from. We are fortunately beginning to pass away from what Professor Edwin Holt has called the "bead theory" of origin and causation to what is now called the "functional or reciprocal theory." Great events, and especially great personalities, are not strung along like successive beads on a string, each one the antecedent of the next. New events and personalities are always in reciprocal relation to their past and their future, not in a relationship of mere consequent to antecedent. What is about to dawn, what is about to be born, often comes to sudden light in an event or in a great person, though the past was unconscious of the dawning future until the unique moment through some unique person revealed it. The event flashes out the unrecognized tendency of the past, just as one suddenly discovers what he has all along *meant*. In a very real way the great genius is a vital junction of a past that was and a future that is to be.

We shall never discover the real St. Francis by reducing *The Mirror of Perfection*, the *Lives* by Thomas of Celano, and *The Little Flowers* to bare facts that can be historically verified and which are got by eliminating all that partakes of the marvelous and wonderful, for he was just the kind of person who made everybody expect the wonderful and marvelous. It is no accident that poetry and art seized upon him and enveloped him in their magnificent glory. He must have been the kind of person who could do what he did. He was the kind of person that made his successors interpret him as they did, think of him as they did, feel toward him as they did. We cannot find him at any cross-section of time. He was a reciprocal junction between a past and a future and he reveals the future even more than he does the past.

We cannot estimate the life and experience of Jesus alone by discovering what name He used for Himself, or what title His disciples applied to Him. It is interesting to answer such questions, and they are important as far as they go, but they do not go to the core of the matter. It is His type of life which most concerns us, His experience of God, His way of translating love into action. And I am convinced that St. Paul and St. John, who interpret His life, His spirit, His dynamic influence to us, are as truly *sources* for His portrait as are the synoptic Gospels.

I have been contending that Christianity began in a novel experience of God. It was originally a way of life, an exhibition and practice of love and spiritual power. I do not care for the moment whether we shall call this experience, this way of life, "mysticism," or not. It is not, of course, what has historically and technically been called by that word. But it was, above everything else, the flooding in of the Life of God, a release of new spiritual energies, the first-hand discovery of new forces to live by, of new powers for the spiritual conquest of the world. It is the greatest instance of it in human history, and the succeeding instances are paler, thinner repetitions of, or attempts to return to, this primitive life and experience. It is a nice question, what it is that makes certain persons so dynamic? How can one individual shift the line of march for the whole race? Why does such immense energy burst in just at this special point and raise the level of humanity in a unique degree?

My next question has to do with organization. Did the organization of the Church spring out of the Christian experience? Was the organization penetrated with the new experience? Did it tend to propagate the experience, to keep it fresh and alive, and to pass it on as a vital thing? Or did it tend to arrest it and produce something static? There was an early stage during which, in some true sense, organization and experience mutually assisted each other. I hope later to come back to consider the character of the earliest organization of Christianity. But another type of organization and system soon superseded and obliterated the simple life-forms of the early high-tide period, and out of it developed, through the Latin genius, the most imperial system of organization the world has ever seen. Fortunately this historical system has often given opportunity—sometimes in spite of itself—for the birth of new vital experiences, for fresh incursions of the Life of God, and for the winds of the Spirit to blow as they listed. But for the most part, the organization has been concerned to expand, perfect, maintain, safeguard, and exalt itself, because those who composed the Church soon came to believe that it was indispensable for man's salvation, and essential for the transmission of the grace of God revealed in Christ. It quickly became a substitute for the experience of God, for the way of life, for the Kingdom of God, for the living sense of the divine presence and power of the Spirit.

It traveled away from and missed the heart and substance of Christ's religion of life. A theological Christ took the place of the great Galilean, while a church theory and a system of services became substitutes for the thrill of fellowship with a divine Companion. The theological battles over the metaphysical nature of Christ and over His relation to God the Father are among the most amazing facts of history. These battles were concerned not with the Galilean Jesus but with a Greek theory of the Logos. The great constructions of the system-builders dealt not with the New Testament God, or Christ, or Holy Spirit, but with metaphysical theories and abstractions which had long been battle issues for Greek dialectics. The systems, in short, did not grow out of Christian experience, nor were they founded on experience. They were the elaborate constructions of abstract logic.

Once more I am not crying out against the strange curvature and loops of ancient history. The spiritual faiths of humanity must be expressed in terms of prevailing thought, and it was essential that the Christian faith should discover how to express itself in the current thought of the Hellenic mind. Only we ought not to suppose that this expression is something sacred and final. Much rather we ought to be concerned to have our present-day interpretations fit our own experience and our own clearest ideas of reality and our highest ideals of life. These formulations were logical constructions, and the mental acceptance of approved theories came in many minds to be a "substitute" for an experience of God and for Christ's way of life.

In somewhat the same way, though with much less conscious guidance, theories of heaven and hell became "substitutes" for a religion of life and experience. The shift of focus from this world to the world beyond was well underway in all quarters in the first century. The Jewish Apocalypses reveal the tendency. The widespread Gnostic movements show its sweep and strength. The immense interest in Mystery Religions is part of the same concern, and the absorbing passion for ascetic practices and painful ways of life here below makes it very evident that Christianity came into a world that was at heart deeply pessimistic, and that cared above everything else to find a way of escape to the realm of peace and joy yonder—the real fatherland of the soul.

The deep spiritual message of Christ about the infinite value of life and His insistence that victory, joy, and peace are meant for this world were not sufficient to turn the set of the tide. The note of pessimism went on growing and world-flight became a feature of all religions. Converts to

Christianity brought with them into their new faith a fixed mental climate of despair for this world and a disposition to look for their relief in a kingdom beyond the stars. I heard George Santayana once illustrate the ancient sense of disillusion and despair with this striking figure. This world seemed to them to be a kind of circus hoop filled with tissue paper to be leaped through. St. Ignatius, St. Irenaeus, and Tertullian were great creative personalities who helped by their impressive writings to carry this attitude and tendency into the normal thinking of widespread Christian groups. St. Cyprian, a noble figure and a brave martyr, raised the same mood to a higher intensity, and with St. Anthony and St. Jerome the hatred of life here and the passion for peace and safety yonder came full flood into the Christian Church.

No one person in early Christian history can be singled out as responsible for the excessive interest in the life beyond. As I have said, it was a prevailing vogue in the world into which Christianity was born. Perhaps Plato should have a heavier share of the blame for this attitude than any other one person, though the two-world theory, with its tendency to write *this* world down and *that* world up, is due rather to a superficial interpretation of Plato than to Plato's own view of life. In any case it was the background of Greek and Hellenistic thought, not Christ's teaching nor Christian experience, which determined the focus of later Christian aspiration, as it shaped also the Christology of the creeds. When, however, the minds of the creative leaders of Christian thought had once become absorbed with theories of salvation—a salvation which was to be attained and enjoyed in a world beyond this temporal sphere—the natural result was that heaven and hell assumed an importance out of all comparison with any earthly issue or event. It was no accident that the greatest poet between Homer and Shakespeare chose for his theme the domain and condition of the soul after death. I am of course aware that in the deepest sense Dante is concerned with the inherent state of the human soul, with the way in which the dominant love in a man's soul shapes his eternal destiny, but he worked out his conception of "eternal destiny," as Michelangelo also did, in terms of the scenery and circumstance of another world; and that other world is obviously far more important than this one is. Everything turns in the last analysis upon the question of how to escape the torments and how to attain the joys of a future world which infinitely outweighs in value the brief temporal span of the vaporous life here below.

So long as this estimate of values held sway, the supreme problems were bound to be problems of eschatology. Nobody expected the Kingdom of God to be *built* here; it was to be *found* by those who through divine grace and human faith climbed "the steep and rugged path to heaven," which in almost everybody's thought *was* the Kingdom of God. This altered perspective is responsible for many of our tragic Christian defeats. It has become a trite remark that Christianity has not only failed; it has not yet been tried. In a very real sense it is true that it has not been yet tried as a way of life. It has been very seriously tried as a scheme for securing salvation in a new Jerusalem yonder—*la bas*, as the French say. But that is a very different thing from trying it as a spring and energy of daily life in this world. Almost every major spiritual cause has suffered on account of this other-world focus and perspective. War and human bloodshed have been accepted as a necessary feature of this world which is the unhappy domain of fallen man. Here primitive instincts must have their fling, but yonder peace and love will reign in *sæculum sæculorum*. Wrong social and economic conditions have been accepted and allowed to go on unchallenged because we do not expect an ideal state of things here; that is to come in the soul's eternal paradise. This subtle pessimism about man's inherent nature, and about all social, economic, and political systems made up of and controlled by men, has been an age-long drag on the spiritual progress of the race. Under its pernicious influence, we let this world slide along its old slippery grooves of sin and shame, satisfied if we make provision for a few chosen vessels to find their way to the blessed mansions of heavenly rest, while the others are shunted along the path —not always a primrose one—to the everlasting bonfire.

What a difference it would have made if there could have been a body of exuberant and triumphant men and women through all the centuries, bearing witness to the power of the Spirit to raise life to complete health and holiness. There were, no doubt, "saints" in all the periods, but a saint was considered a supernatural phenomenon, not a normal product of Christ's way of life. The theory of total depravity settled down over men's lives like the shadow of a mighty eclipse. There was not much to be expected of beings who had been wrecked root and branch in the catastrophe of the fall. Only by the rarest miracle could the ruin be repaired. This loss of nerve, this age-long inferiority complex at the heart of the race, worked a good deal of havoc. Wherever the Galilean faith and vision about man's divine possibilities broke in and touched here and there a life, it was like a lift of fresh air from another clime. St. Paul declared that "in Jesus Christ the divine 'yes' has sounded forth," but the world in the main continued to live in the eclipse of the everlasting "no" rather than in the radiance of the everlasting "yes."

The deep inward religion of the noblest of the psalms is far superior to this distorted Christian aspiration. The psalmists had almost no vision for another world. Their range, except in a few rare instances, is confined strictly to this present life. What they are to attain and enjoy must be attained and enjoyed here. We may feel regretful sympathy that they could not have had the comfort and inspiration of a larger hope. But at any rate the very limitation of their scope of life gave an extraordinary spiritual intensity to it. There throbs here a passion for God—God for His own sake—such as we seldom find among our more favored Christian groups. "I have no good except *thee*," one of them says; "I have set the Lord always before me: Because He is at my right hand I shall not be greatly moved"; and finally he asserts, "I shall not be moved at all." "In thy presence is fullness of joy." This sense of divine presence, this spirit of trust and confidence, produce an inward calm and poise and power certainly not often paralleled, and we still go back to these ancient saints for our best specimens of a religious experience triumphant over pain, loss, and defeat, and inwardly fortified to stand the universe.

There is one more of these "substitute" tendencies which has worked momentous results and consequence through the long stretch of Christian history. I refer to the immense importance which has attached to the form and authority of the ecclesiastical organization. As soon as the historic theory of salvation swung into first place in men's thoughts, the ecclesiastical organization became an inherent feature of it. It was a deep-rooted faith everywhere by the end of the first century that sacraments which imparted the divine life to the faithful partaker of them were essential to salvation. It is not our problem at the present moment to discover how this remarkable idea arose and spread. It is enough to note that it appears in many lands and in many religions and that very early in the life of the Christian Church it was naïvely accepted as a vital aspect of the new faith.

The impassioned Epistles of St. Ignatius, written on his way to Rome where he was condemned to die in the Colosseum, call the eucharist the medicine of immortality, and baptism the medicinal bath of regeneration. If sacraments were to be effective in this supernatural manner, it meant at once that the Church must be miraculously endowed through its ordained priests to work such tremendous effects. So, too, as soon as soundness of doctrine rose to a place of first importance for salvation, as it did in the struggle with Gnosticism, it was felt that there must be some authoritative body endowed with divine power to discern and preserve and transmit "the faith once delivered." Then again, if the theory of Heaven and Hell and still more the slightly later theory of Purgatory were to be effective, it necessarily involved some authoritative earthly administration of the entrance conditions. Someone must be entrusted with the keys. Someone must have the dread power to loose and bind, to open and shut.

The gradual development of this august and imperial ecclesiastical system was thus not an accident. It was essential to the whole conception of salvation, and it is an inherent and organic part of the Church as St. Ignatius, St. Irenaeus, Tertullian, St. Cyprian and St. Augustine, its early builders, conceived it—as a divine *instrument of salvation*.

Quite obviously, therefore, we do not have, in the historic Church, organizations and systems that have sprung mainly out of and been born from first-hand *experience* of God. The systems which I have been reviewing have their roots in great world movements of ancient times. Every land has made its contribution. Every contemporary religion added its rill to the growing stream. Plato and Aristotle were apostles along with Peter and James and John. Philo and Plotinus all unconsciously helped to lay the pillars of this mighty structure. Alexander the Great and the Caesars of the Empire had their share in building the imperial system that supplanted them. There is nowhere any greater work of genius than this. It was the work of ages. It fitted the mental outlook and deep-lying aspirations of its period. It disciplined the pagan races. It produced glorious saints. It inspired art and literature. It preserved and transmitted the Scriptures. It had something in its wide mother-breast for every type of individual mind and spirit, and we cannot speak lightly of its splendid mission.

The Reformation brought a profound change both in the form and content of Christianity. The new type which emerged was what biologists call a "mutation." It was not the old amended and modified at a few specific points; it was something novel and unique. It not only looked different on the outside, but it had a different inward feel. There was a fresh return to the New Testament model and there was born also a new kind of religious experience which was quite unlike that of the pious worshiper under the old system. But in spite of all this, the main line reformers did not succeed in producing an organization or a system of thought taken either from the New Testament or developed out of their own religious experience. There was a short, heroic period in Luther's life during which he gave immense scope to the living, creative faith which made him a reformer, and he seemed ready to reconstruct the Church outwardly and inwardly so that it might conform to his freshly discovered principles of spirit and freedom. There were high moments when he conceived of the new Church that was being formed as a community of believers, each member being a spiritual priest. "I believe," he wrote, "that there is on earth, wide as the world, only one holy universal Christian church which is nothing else than the community or congregation of the saints." He seems to be thinking here of a mighty spiritual organism or group life, always dynamic and capable of constant growth and inward transformation.

But Luther had to deal with a network and a tangle of complication. The radical wing pushed his principles of freedom to a far extreme. The peasants threatened to overthrow the established economic and political order. Those who represented the moral and intellectual forces behind the Reformation were conservative. They would stand for certain changes but they would go only so far, and there they held the line rigidly. The result was that the great principle of individualism, of freedom, of personal faith, and of a communion of spiritual believers each contributing to the life of all, quickly gave place to a stiff church system, with doctrine raised to a pitch of importance that had been unknown in the old Church.

It was Calvin's aim and mission to develop a Church organization and to formulate a theological system which would compete on its own ground with the Roman Catholic Church. His work has all the marks of creative genius. It was an almost unparalleled feat of construction. Calvinism soon became the outstanding form of Protestant Christianity and it became one of the mightiest forces of modern history. But it would be quite impossible to maintain that the vast system of theology or the solid structure of organization had much relation to immediate experience. Calvin's method was logical interpretation of the Bible, especially of the Hebrew Commonwealth set forth in the old Testament and taken to be the infallible word of God for all the ages —the pattern in the Mount—according to which model every feature of the Church system was to be constructed. This habit of mind grew stronger and sterner with the followers of Calvin, who were smaller, narrower men, and there came out of this work of genius a very long list of major and minor tragedies. I have been dealing, as one sees, with Christian organizations and systems which have sprung from world-movements that had little or nothing to do with the inward spiritual experience of individual believers, or which, as in the case of Calvin, have been constructed out of a theory of Scripture that made the commonwealth of Israel, before the exile, the model for a Church in the sixteenth century A. D. This, again, had little or nothing to do with the inner life of the believer himself.

The revolts from the great systems of thought and organization have unfortunately usually been in the direction of somewhat dry and thin rationalisms. The deists and many other "revolters," before and since, have tried to find relief from stiff and elaborate historical systems by constructing a rationalistic theology or a positivistic religion. But these creations are all too "icily regular" for the full life and expansion of the human spirit. Rationalisms never minister to the whole of a man and they always produce a reaction in the direction of emotionalism or sentimentalism. The "other half" of life that was neglected asserts its rights and has its short reign. But it, too, is a half and not a whole. History reveals a zigzag line of revolts tacking back and forth from rationalism to romanticism and then again to a new rationalism. There is no final solution ever until man's whole life finds scope for itself, until the deeper springs are liberated and brought into play, as well as the pure intellect. We need to find a way of life that will give the mind its full scope and which at the same time will call into action the subtle, hidden, more or less inarticulate spiritual forces in us which carry us out beyond what we see or touch or think.

Now I am ready to turn to the other side, the positive aspect of my subject. I want now to see if we can find some suggestive instances of direct correspondence between religious experience and its expression in forms of thought and organization. And then I propose to consider in what ways and through what forms mystical experience can best transmit its discoveries and its life. I want to see a Church that carries on the accumulated gains of history and art, that ministers with wisdom and insight to man's deep yearning for immortal life, that speaks with spiritual authority about the way of salvation and the nature of it, but I want also a Church that has an effective way of helping seekers find God here and now, where we need Him most, and which is at the same time dedicated to the task of building the kingdom of peace and love in the towns and cities of the modern world.

CHAPTER V

My previous chapter contended that the organization and polity of the historic Church did not have their ground in the nature and demands of religious experience. They did not essentially spring out of religious needs. They were taken over very largely from existing faiths and forms, and adapted to fit the slowly maturing purposes of the builders of the imperial Church.

That Church, even with and in spite of its elaborate ritual, its authoritative creeds, and its potent ecclesiasticism, was notwithstanding, throughout its long history, a nursery of mystics. Even the greatest of the Church builders were themselves mystics—St. Augustine, St. Gregory the Great, and St. Bernard of Clairvaux. This constant recurrence of the tendency to find God by a direct inward way is certainly an august testimony to the spiritual depth of man's nature. He cannot live by schemes and systems alone any more than he can by bread. Fortunately, the

Church always recognized the importance of the inward way, and made it easy, with its wise inclusiveness, for individual souls to have their quiet Bethel experiences. As it built chapels for the cult of widely diverse saints and promoted pilgrimages to these different shrines, so also it encouraged the mystic to make his daring pilgrimage in quest, not of relics and outward tokens, but of God Himself. The mystic who was approved in the historic Church was, however, always an individual mystic. His business was to find the interior way to God. He went about his quest without disturbing anyone else. He did not follow the habit of the Hebrew prophets and cry out against the system that had nurtured him. He was satisfied to have his undisturbed opportunity to seek and find, and he was a welcome worshiper so long as he refrained from counter-organization. This long-continued historic situation has encouraged the prevailing opinion that mysticism is essentially a private and individual affair. William James fell in with this line of thought in his famous definition of religion as "the feelings, acts, and experiences of *individual men in their solitude*, so far as they apprehend themselves to stand in relation to whatever they may consider the divine."

Walt Whitman in his *Democratic Vistas* says the same thing, emphatically and in beautiful style:

> I should say that only in the perfect uncontamination and solitariness of individuality may the spirituality of religion positively come forth at all. Only here, and on such terms, the meditation, the devout ecstasy, the soaring flight. Only here, communion with the mysteries, the eternal problems, whence? whither? alone, and identity, and the mood—and the soul emerges, and all statements, churches, sermons, melt away like vapors. Alone, and silent thought and awe, and aspiration, and then the interior consciousness, like a hitherto unseen inscription, in magic ink, beams out its wondrous lines to the sense. Bibles may convey, and priests expound, but it is exclusively for the noiseless operation of one's isolated self, to enter the pure ether of veneration, reach the divine levels, and commune with the unutterable.

I maintain that the solitary character of mysticism is not due to the essential nature of it, but only to the peculiar circumstance that the type of organization which existed in the Church forced it, in the main, to confine itself to an individualistic form. I am convinced, as I shall proceed to show, that mysticism flourishes best in a group, and that it can, if left to itself, produce out of its experience a type of organization that favors its growth and increase in depth and power.

The mystic is a person who feels himself to be possessed of more than one effective way of dealing with what is deepest and most real in the universe. We have made great progress with our efforts to bring our world into an ordered rational system, and there are many aspects of it which submit perfectly to the categories of mathematical science. But there are other aspects which do not easily fit into those categories, or which fit only after great reductions have been made from the actual data of experience. Whenever rationalism has been overpressed, as it was, for example, in the eighteenth century; whenever it assumes to take the whole road, there is always a vigorous reaction and the other extreme pendulum-swing follows in the direction of those inarticulate aspects of our life which we call feelings, emotions, and sentiments. In the long run, the deeper wisdom of the race asserts itself and insists upon *the rights of the whole self* as against a one-sided emphasis of either head or heart.

There is obviously a vast and very important residuum left over after what we call the intellect, our cognitive capacity, has exhausted all its available efforts to rationalize, organize, and describe what is real. The *limit* is reached at a number of points, and yet there is something beyond each one of the cognitive limits which immensely concerns us. All our knowledge-trails stop at a terminus before the true goal of life is attained. We only know in part, and we may as well humbly recognize that the way of cognition will never carry us to the end of our quest.

The implications which attach to all our stages of knowledge force us to ask whether there is not something in us like the marvelous antennae of insects that can feel out beyond the limiting barriers and discover what the beyond is like. The mystic is gifted with powers for such discovery. He feels a contact with what lies out beyond the world of eyes and ears and finger-tips, though it is by means of his entire integrated self, rather than by some mysterious sense or instinct, that he operates. He catches swift flashes of insight which *reveal*. By strict discipline of spirit and by refining processes that make his soul peculiarly sensitive, he reacts to spiritual currents which others miss. He receives what seem like incursions from beyond the margins of knowledge, and he lives out beyond those margins in ways of response and relationship, which convince him that the knowledge-circle lies within great concentric rings of spiritual reality waiting to be explored. The spectrum has its ultra-red and its ultra-violet rays which are just as real as red or violet, though we cannot *see* them; and there are sane, rational persons who believe that they can, in a similar way, extend the domain of their life experiences out beyond the frontiers of that region within which sense-knowledge feels at home.

It is not alone in the sphere of religion that these "swift flashes of insight" reach beyond the beaten track which the intellect has made. Einstein has recently said that without intuition the highest achievements in mathematics could not have been made. The experiences and discoveries of Descartes, Sir Isaac Newton, and Sir William Rowan Hamilton finely illustrate this point. Science has a long list of forward steps that were made possible by sudden flashes of intuition, and the story of invention contributes also its quota of such incidents. There are many forms of experience in which wholes are grasped without any conscious process of building the whole up out of parts. The mind leaps to a higher synthesis without noting any *steps*.

Mysticism in the sphere of religion is a persistent testimony to a realm of reality that supplements and fulfills the inadequate realm which we have explored, and therefore call the "natural." I have used the unfortunate word "beyond," but it always turns out to be a fact that the "beyond" is *here* as truly as it is yonder, just as gravitation is found to be revealed in and through any given matter, though it always transcends it. Part of our retina, the outer rim of it, is without color-cones of vision and can report only shades of gray. Many persons have an entire retina like that outer rim and they are color-blind. They have ground for insisting that gray is the only color in the universe. But some of us —this time most of us—know better. Glossy purples are just as real as grays. But if only one person in a million saw colors, and had their hearts leap up when they beheld the rainbow in the sky, the rest would insist that the color-seers were pathological and indulged in *Schwärmerei* and auto-suggestion! Some less favored persons lack certain delicate adjustments in the organ of Corti in the inner ear and so fail to enjoy the higher ranges of music. They are frankly bored by an orchestra and greatly prefer solitude and quiet to the most perfect symphony. It says nothing to them and carries them to no levels of reality. For other better endowed individuals, music opens doors into the infinite; it adds a new dimension to the world. It is one of the most marvelous of all the overbrimming experiences of our life. But how does it work its spells of joyous enchantment? Not by argument or demonstration; not by some compelling power of common logic and proof. Music, as we have seen, cannot be rationalized and made cogent and coercive for all minds. The soul in music arrives at the goal without knowing how the journey was made.

Here is the finger of God, a flash of the will that can,
Existent behind all laws, that made them, and lo, they are!
And I know not if, save in this, such gift be allowed
    to man,
That out of three sounds he frame, not a fourth sound,
    but a star.
Consider it well: each tone of our scale in itself is nought;
It is everywhere in the world—loud, soft, and all is said;
Give it to me to use! I mix it with two in my thought:
And there! You have heard and seen: consider and bow
    the head!

Those mystics whom I have called "sane and rational," though, of course, it is a very bold and adventurous kind of sanity and rationalism! are mystics who make claim only to what they have verified as having life-value for spiritual ends. They do not traffic in the weird and occult. They do not profess to have private and esoteric information. They are not purveyors of secret mysteries. They are only concerned, if possible, to be living, sensitive, responsive organs of that deepest Life who is the Life of all our lives.

This type of experience will, of course, be very different in different periods of history. It is, as I have said, the response and reaction of the total self, not of some isolated fraction or "faculty" of it, not some "unexplored hinterland" of the self; and consequently it will be influenced by the intellectual climate of the time, by the dominant modes of feeling and sentiment, and by the urges and expectant attitudes which are in vogue. I think it can be shown that mystical religion is as dependent on group life, on literature, on previous and contemporary experience, as any other form of religion is or as a man's concrete conscience is. It is not born like a parentless Melchizedec. "Not in utter nakedness, not in entire forgetfulness," does it come from God. Carlyle rightly insisted that "the inward Life of mankind is the same in no two ages." There are "fashions" in the field of mysticism as truly as there are in clothes or automobiles.

At the same time, there are certain persistent habits and fundamental traits which characterize the experience in all times and in all lands. Suggestion, expectation, influence of mystical books, contact with other mystics, are the powerful human agencies which tend to prepare a person for such an experience; probably though, in the last analysis, the psychical disposition of the individual himself is the crucial factor. It comes only to those who can meditate, who can stop living by clock-time and space-speeds, and center down into that interior hush where the human spirit touches the skirts of God.

With these introductory considerations, we are now ready to take up the question of the type of organization and polity which fits best with mystical religion. It can flourish in almost any external system, if that system is elastic enough to allow fairly free sub-organization to exist within the larger inclusive framework. That has been the case in the Roman Catholic Church, in the Mohammedan faith, and in some of the religious systems of India, though the most intense and "contagious" forms of mysticism have appeared in *mutation periods* of history, times of yeast and ferment, when the steadying fly-wheel of organized authority had slowed down. Under conditions of that sort, mystical movements show a pretty well-defined tendency and form.

The primitive Church, in its earliest stages, presents a very interesting outbreak of mystical experience, and at the same time it exhibits those peculiar organizing tendencies which are, I think, typical of a pronounced mystical "emergence." Whatever else the Pentecost event may have been, it was certainly a birth-moment of the Church and it was obviously a profound mystical experience in which a large group of expectant persons had the consciousness of invasion. If it is never *easy* to trace the history of the visible Church, it is quite *impossible* to write the history of the invisible Church, or to tell in the coinage of speech what is surging in the hidden deeps of men's hearts in great epoch-moments. Unfortunately, we have no first-hand account of Pentecost, no intimate autobiographical details of it, but Luke's narrative is, of all things, vivid and realistic. The auditions of rushing wind, the photisms seen resting on the head of each, and the ecstatic tongue-speaking which burst forth are all characteristic marks of an intense and emotionally wrought-up group. These things have, one

or all, many times recurred in mystical groups
and usually attend experiences which sweep the
sympathetic nervous system with strong bodily
reverberation and resonance. But the real event
lies deeper. The surrounding spectators were
mainly interested in the superficial phenomena.
The spiritual historian across the centuries is concerned with the incursion or upwelling of an un-
wonted energy—which plainly occurred—the
flooding-in of currents of divine Life. The little
group of believers here passed over from fellowship with an external Companion, whom they had
called Master and whom they had hoped was
Messiah, to the consciousness of an inward spiritual Presence and Power revealed in their own
souls. The experience, common to each believer
there, of new currents of Life breaking in at once
produced an unusual group-consciousness. The
Koinonia, or fellowship of unity, emerged. In
Josiah Royce's phrase, "the community of the
Holy Spirit" was now born.[1]

There is no more mystery about spiritual
Power breaking into and flooding through a person's life than there is about electricity breaking
through a dynamo, or about ether vibrations com-

[1] Streeter's *The Spirit*; Scott's chapter, "What Happened at
Pentecost"; Royce's *The Problem of Christianity*.

ing through a radio set. It is, after all, a question of fact. There can, I think, be no doubt that almost all the early groups of Christians believed that a divine Spirit, which they often identified with the invisible Christ, did thus break into their lives and give them their new dynamic and "the fruits of the Spirit." The testinmony reached its supreme emphasis in St. Paul. It is everywhere in his writings a current idea, and it was undoubtedly born of experience. Christ present in the midst of His little fellowship, Christ with His followers even unto the end of the world, was both promise and experience. Whether in Jerusalem, Antioch, Galatia, Corinth, or Ephesus, it can be taken as certain that the little *ecclesia* of believers felt themselves fused into a community of the Spirit and swept by some measure of that invading Life which came first upon the little circle in the upper room in Jerusalem. The invasion of the Spirit and the fusing of the fellowship, together with the signs and fruits of the Spirit, were the necessary credentials that an *ecclesia* group was born. There was a band of disciples in Ephesus before St. Paul came there, but they did not form an *ecclesia* in St. Paul's sense, until "the Holy Spirit came upon them," and then "they spake with tongues and prophesied," like the other church groups.[2]

While this mystical stage of primitive Christianity lasted, the fellowship, or *koinonia*, was an organism rather than an organization. The members had a common experience. They were *fused*. They were baptized into *one* Spirit. They ate a community meal, all partaking together of one loaf, and all together drinking of one cup. This love-meal, at least in its high-tide period, was eaten with an awakened memory of Christ's last meal with His friends, and with a fresh, palpitating sense of His invisible presence now with them. It was both sacramental and mystical in the true sense, and it was a powerful integrating experience. There was no rigid system. There were no technical officials. "Custom" laid no heavy hand upon anyone. Routine and sacred order had not come yet. There was large scope for spontaneity and personal initiative. Persons and gifts counted for everything. Procedure was fluid and not yet pattern-stamped and standardized. There was place for the independent variable. "The fellowship" was more like a family group than like what *we* call a church. Love, rather than rules, guided it. Everything was

[2] Acts xix. 1-7.

unique and nothing repeatable. The exercises, if we may judge by the glimpses we get from Acts and Corinthians, were of a sort that would favor mystical experience, while at the same time they were largely born out of and developed to fit personal and community experiences. No leader dominated the group meetings. No program was essential. The little body met as a community of the Spirit; and, as St. Paul said, "Where the Spirit is, there is liberty"—not bondage or routine. The exercises were charismatic, that is, due to the display of "spiritual gifts" possessed by those who were present. The leading "gift" was prophecy, which consisted of the spontaneous utterance of a message believed to be inspired by the Spirit, or directly given in words or vision by the Spirit. It was rapturous and ecstatic speaking rather than carefully prepared and rationally ordered speaking, and when it came from persons of rich experience who were highly endowed and who had formed a well-stored subconscious life to draw from, it was often illuminating and constructive—"edifying," as St. Paul would say. Sometimes the flooded lives broke forth in hymns; sometimes they all together ejaculated words like "Abba" or "Maranatha," or "groanings that could not be uttered"; and sometimes one or more broke forth into emotionally loaded, unutterable utterance, that is, tongue-speaking.

This sounds chaotic and unedifying, and much of it was so as always happens when an intensive wave of enthusiasm breaks over groups of people, but there was also a strain of another type persistently present in it. There was a greatly heightened moral power. They walked in the Spirit and they bore the fruits of the Spirit: love, joy, peace, long-suffering, kindness, goodness, faithfulness, meekness, self-control. St. Paul's picture, in I Cor. vi. 9-11, shows like a flash of lightning what their lives had been before they were "washed and sanctified"; and in his epistle to them he calls them "letters of Jesus Christ written by the Holy Spirit, being transformed into His image from glory to glory by the Spirit of the Lord." He, at least, *expects* them to live in a spirit of coöperative love which is patient, kind, long-suffering, gentle, unprovoked, which believeth, hopeth and endureth everything, and which, as an inward-working constructive force, would make them a single body, a unified fellowship.

This, I take it, was the original idea of the Church. It was a spiritual fellowship. It was an organic body held together by a common experi-

ence and by internal forces of life. It was guided
by gifted persons rather than by technical officials.
Its exercises had a large degree of spontaneity.
Its sacraments were vital, refreshing, and unify-
ing. Its driving power was a consciousness of the
Spirit, and its entire method of organization
tended to promote inward mystical experience.
It was a mystical group, and the body of the
membership was thought of as an organ of the
Spirit—"you are Christ's body."[3]

This was a Pauline ideal. It was never fully
realized, and it was, in any case, only a short-
time experiment. Other and quite different theories of organization were pushing into operation
from the very first. Jewish systems, Greek systems, Roman systems, Gnostic cults, Mystery Religions, were all part of the air men breathed.
The Church could conquer only by absorbing.
The transformation was rapid, and the new order
with its rigid framework and its potency for imperial sway was well in sight before the canon of
the New Testament was closed.

The forms of mysticism which came into Christianity from the outstanding Greek mystic,
Plotinus, were individualistic in type. St. Augustine and Pseudo-Dionysius were the two Christian

[3] I Cor. xii. 27.

founders of this form of mysticism. It was an intellectual, not an emotional type. It was founded on the inherent capacity of the soul (Mind), rather than upon the inrush of an environing Spirit. It was restrained, refined, noncharismatic, and an experience of "the alone with the Alone." It came to beautiful flower in the lives of the Victorines and of Bernard of Clairvaux.

In the early thirteenth century there began to appear again sporadic outbreaks of group-mysticism. The influences which led to it are obscure. The writings of John Scotus Erigena, the Arabian commentaries on Aristotle, subterranean currents from early Montanism, and the New Testament are certainly some of the springs which fed it. It took the form of intimate fellowships. It was inspirational and charismatic. These mystics once more felt themselves to be organs of the divine Spirit. They spoke and wrote under inspiration, and they felt that external forms were "dead," and that the Life of God revealed within the soul was the all-important matter. There was a great variety of such movements, but all of them took the form of fellowships or brotherhoods. Organization was minimal. Life, freedom, spirit, friendship, and spontaneity were everything. They lived in groups and fostered their spiritual life through community silence, prayer, and loving service. These group movements grew and developed for more than a hundred years, and reached their climax in the Friends of God and the Brethren of the Common Life. These movements produced some of the noblest mystical literature in existence, for instance, *Theologia Germanica* and the *Imitation of Christ*. These two books follow, in large measure, the beaten track of Catholic mysticism —"the alone with the Alone." But there is another great collection of mystical literature of a semi-fictitious sort produced anonymously by the Rhine groups of the Friends of God. These books all show a definite *tendency*—the exaltation of lay-religion, the importance of humility and purity of heart, the fact that God directly teaches the responsive soul, and that experience of God is the essential mark of Christian life. These little fourteenth-century books, now preserved in the Strasbourg library, reveal a simple form of mystical Christianity which makes everything of direct contact with God and nothing at all of externals. These Christians were members of the Church, but their real life was in their "brotherhood nests," as John Tauler called them, their retreats where they enjoyed fellowship, practiced silence and communion together, produced their imaginative books to interpret their faith and experience, and where once more they exhibited the ideals of the original Christian communities.

These Friends of God attained a high level of everyday living, and they seem to have shared the aspiration of one of their noblest interpreters: "To be to the eternal God what a man's hand is to a man." "The Friend of God from the Oberland" is the ideal figure of the group. He is almost certainly a literary creation, and all the more for that reason he presents their loftiest spiritual ideals. John Tauler was, on the other hand, a flesh and blood man who wrought out in a very hard epoch, and in the rough circumstances of a medieval city in time of plague and interdict, a nearly perfect life of devotion and service. He was a good specimen of the practical mystic who translated all his experiences of God into deeds of life, and who declared that "no virtue is to be trusted until it has been put into practice." Here we have, then, once more a vital mysticism, producing an extensive literature, nurturing very noble souls, flourishing at a high pitch for at least half a century, maintaining a simple, fluid, fellowship-type of organization, favorable to personal communion and corporate silence, where each helped the other to be an organ of the Eternal Goodness.

The Society of Friends offers, perhaps, the best historical example, especially in its formative period, of a mystical body with an organization adapted to promote mystical experience in its membership. George Fox, the founder of it, was in many points, both in disposition and experience, like Jacob Boehme of Silesia, though he was a simpler type of man, fortunately freed from the heavy inheritance of alchemy, and much more gifted with leadership and organizing capacity. His mystical experiences gave him absolute assurance of direct divine contact; and under what he felt to be illuminations, or "openings" from God, he formulated a simple, experimental type of Christianity. It was based primarily on the faith that God and man are essentially interrelated, that there is something of God in man's inmost being, and that all men, and women too, may become revealers of the Life and Spirit of God.

He proposed to purify and simplify Protestant Christianity by discounting its externals, by going over from outward authority to inward authority, and by demonstrating the fact that salvation is

the work of an inward spirit and power—an affair
of life and experience—rather than the effect of
believing a system of theology. The disciples
and followers who gathered around him were,
for the most part, mystical-minded persons who
had been through a long discipline of waiting and
seeking for inward light and power. Isaac Penington, one of the rarest and most beautiful characters of the early group who has been quoted
in a former chapter, declared when his great
experience broke upon his soul: "This is He, this
is He. There is no other. This is He whom I
have waited for and sought after from my childhood. I have met with my God; I have met with
my Saviour. I have felt the healings drop upon
my soul from under His wings." Here, again, is
a charming bit from Francis Howgill: "Why
gad you abroad? Why trim you with the Saints'
words when you are ignorant of the life? Return, return to Him who is the first love, and the
firstborn of every creature. . . . Return home to
within: sweep your houses all: the groat [the lost
coin] is there."[4] Not only the leaders and prop-
agators—"publishers of truth," as they were
called—but the simple yeoman folk who re-
sponded in large numbers to the new and danger-

[4] *A Lamentation for the Scattered Tribes*, 1656.

ous message felt, as Fox did, that they "knew God experimentally" and had "a key that did open." It was a religion of inward experience and enabled men to have the conviction that God and the soul were unsundered.

The organization which sprang out of this experimental faith, and for which Fox himself was largely responsible, was admirably suited to its needs and its aims. It was organic rather than something constructed. It was a growth of life rather than a pattern-scheme. The biologists have coined the word "symbiosis," which means a group association of insects—ants or bees—living together in harmony and coöperation, instinctively fused together into one social whole. The early Society of Friends, or "Children of the Light," as they first called themselves, was a "symbiosis." It was a creation of unconscious insight, of unpremeditated intuition. It was a spiritual fellowship assisting each individual member to increase in depth and scope of life, and at the same time steadily becoming more coherently integrated.

The responsibility for the life and welfare of the whole was distributed over the entire membership. There was no visible head—no priest, no vicar, no cure of souls, no president, no chairman—just a fellowship of persons seeking to form a living organism through which the Life of God could reveal itself. There were no fixed beliefs which had to be accepted; no sacred ways which had to be followed; no pattern ritual to be recited; no external sacraments to be performed; no set sermons to be preached; no formal prayers to be prayed; no benediction to be pronounced. Each person worshiped for himself, and felt that if he was to find God and have his heart burn with the real presence he must himself prepare the way for that great consummation. But it soon came to be discovered that, where many together in hush and silence were seeking for direct communion and companionship with God, each one helped all the rest. They somehow lent their souls out to produce a corporate state which in its unity was immensely more than the sum of the parts. If one found God, it helped them all to find God. This novel worship-meeting was, at its truest and best, a mystical group, often a spiritually baptized and inwardly fused *whole*. What happens so strikingly in a "team" happened here in this coöperating, "symbiotic" fellowship; they did together what no one perhaps could have done alone. Horace J. Bridges of Chicago has recently said with clear insight: "It is said that they (the Quakers) have no ritual, yet there is no device of the Catholic or any other church more penetratingly powerful than the ritual of social silence."

Their meetings for business, too, were "symbiotic," and they still are. The problem, the project, or concern is laid before the meeting and is considered for a period in silence while thought and judgment are being matured. The speaking which follows is spontaneous and free. Various aspects get presented. Then the speaking begins to focus toward one or more conclusions. There is displayed a spirit of give and take. Someone presents a unifying position around which the varying views can coördinate. Gradually the speaking merges toward a central position, and finally the clerk sums up "the sense of the meeting" in a "minute," which the meeting accepts as its conclusion. If no such harmony prevails or can be attained, the clerk's "minute" states that through lack of unity "way does not open to proceed," and the project is turned over to a committee to be further studied and considered and brought back, perhaps in altered form, at the next meeting.

This organic method is very different from the unity of a crowd or a mob. It is a unity made by the intelligent contributions of many coöperating minds and wills. In the process each one comes to be more than himself, and he discovers, too, what he really wants, a thing which he could not discover by himself alone. He and the others together have reached a point which none of them could have reached alone.

This new mysticism wrought out with others is not "a flight of the alone to the Alone," not a moveless ecstasy in which the lonely soul attains a passive union with a super-reality yonder. It is a vital discovery of the divine Life revealing itself here and now in and through a group of persons who are bent on transmitting that Life. It is mysticism not of solitude and self-seeking; it is practical mysticism of life and action. God is not sought as an Infinite beyond all finites, but rather as the inward sap of a living Vine where His life and our lives bear spiritual fruit together.

Quaker humanitarian work, too, has always been a mystical service. It is much more than "charity" or "philanthropy." It is a sharing of life with others. It is a service in which understanding and love penetrate the contribution that is made with an unmistakable perfume. But no less marked is the religious implication of it. It is always *felt* to be something divinely led and

guided—something God Himself is doing through
the human hands that do it. The plans for it are
matured in a *religious* atmosphere and spirit.
The groups which work them out together begin
in silent meditation and look for guidance and
higher light as they proceed; and through all the
work, with its complications and difficulties, there
is an underlying sense of fellowship with God as
the spring and life of it all. So that Quaker humanitarian work—that of John Woolman, Elizabeth Fry, and the extensive relief in Europe since
1914—is as much a part of the Quaker mysticism
as the meeting for worship is. It was religious
experience translated into life and deed. In all
these cases, the organization has emerged from
the life itself and has fitted the needs and apti-
tudes of the life. It has been an organism-type
rather than something adventitious and artificially
imposed. Its duration was brief in the early
Church. It lasted much longer in the fourteenth-
century groups, and it has gone on for two hundred and fifty years in the Society of Friends.

The ideal mystical group, then, is one in which
each member is palpitantly sensitive to the divine
Life, and at the same time all the members fuse
together to form a unified body that heightens and
enhances the spiritual capacity of each—"one un-

divided soul of many a soul." It would be, in a small way, like the famous Igdrasil tree, a living coöperative body, inwardly vital and outwardly fruitful; in short, like the tree of life, perpetually yielding fruit and all the time putting forth healing leaves for the world. It may be a dream that there should be such a Church—a Patmos vision —but there have been actual approaches to it, successful experiments in that general direction; and perhaps, in some favored time, there *may be* such a Church of the Spirit, such a spiritual "symbiosis!"

CHAPTER VI

THE TESTIMONY OF THE SOUL

MODERN philosophy began its great career mainly concerned with the inward drama of the soul. Descartes started with the testimony of self-consciousness. Whatever else may be false, deceptive, or illusory, I cannot doubt my own existence as a thinking subject. Even when I doubt or question, I am nevertheless conscious of *myself* as doubting or questioning. There is one reality that resists all attempts to doubt it, namely, my own consciousness. I am a veritable actor, even though I may only dream the stage, the play, and all the other actors. I am here and I am to be seriously reckoned with. The universe, at least at one point, cannot possibly cut me dead or leave me out of account.

Science, which, along with modern philosophy, owes its basic formulations to Descartes, has tended to travel boldly away from this inward reference. It inclines to dissociate itself from the interior drama and to deal with objective phe-

nomena as though they operated in space and time
without any relationship to mind or any reference to a contemplating subject. They would be
the same, and act the same way, if nobody with
consciousness were there. The field of science is
regarded as strictly impersonal. If the mind is
introduced or implied, it comes in only as specta-
tor and recorder—not as actor. The events of
science are not *dramatic*—they are assumed to be
rigidly mechanical and stubbornly inevitable.

This dual situation—the dramatic character of
self-consciousness on the one hand, and a world
of impersonal phenomena on the other—has con-
stituted the major intellectual problem of the last
three centuries. In the form in which it is usually
put, it becomes at once an insoluble problem.
When one conceives or assumes a free and creative mind playing its rôle as thinker in an unrelated non-spiritual world of matter, there is no
way to bring these two diverse realities into
friendly relationship. In the uncouth words of
Hosea Bigelow:

> They won't nowise wear the ring
> 'Thout years of settin' up and wooin'.

The modern world is floundering about with hopeless inconsistency at the heart of its thinking, with

enfeeblement of will, and with tragic uncertainty, alternating with incursions into shallow and capricious pleasure-seeking. It cannot unite its living and its thinking. No amount of "settin' up and wooin'" will ever bring together in happy union two things that have nothing whatever in common. The only way to arrive at a solution of the mind-matter problem is to cease making the bad start by beginning with two divided abstract entities and, instead, to begin with our rich, concrete, indivisible experience, in which we always find ourselves living in and acting upon a complex situation that transcends our private self as knower. In our actual experience, the mind and the world are in mutual and reciprocal relation. They are already together. They already are in accord and need no wooing to unite them. What fits more perfectly than a mountain sunset and a mind that enjoys it? What union is more complete than a moral will and an external situation which the moral will controls and organizes? Or what is less a dualism than a mind solving a problem of nature?

If we could once get over our habit of treating abstractions as though they were ultimate realities —a habit which the inheritance of three centuries has bred into us—and if we could learn to estimate and value our actual experience in all its range and richness, we might possibly find our way out of the wilderness, where we have been wandering much longer than did the children of Israel on the way to their Promised Land.

The interpretation which science gives us leaves out, by a necessity of its method, just those features of life which are most essential and most important for our human purposes and interests. As soon as we return from our habits of abstraction and focus upon life, upon nature as it is experienced, we find our world full of intrinsic values, situations that have meaning and significance for the development of personality, for the building of the interior self. We discover wholes that are more than the sum of parts. We find a tendency in things to evolve, to form organic wholes, to be dramatic, to reveal their meaning in a larger context, in which aspects come to light that did not appear in the beginning. There is a *principle of concretion and of advance* operating everywhere. Everything we experience has touches of beauty and harmonizes into some larger significant whole. Each event in our experience has expansiveness, points to something more, and so tends to be self-transcendent. If we could carry forward the implications of our concrete experience with the same skill and effectiveness with which we have pushed forward scientific research, we should, I believe, come upon paths that lead straight on to the City of God.

There is a famous treatise of Tertullian's, *On the Testimony of the Soul.* "Whenever the soul comes to itself," he says, "as out of a surfeit, or a sleep or a sickness, and attains something of its natural soundness, it speaks of God." Tertullian wrote that sentence seventeen hundred years ago. Many things which he wrote in that earlier time are not held to be true now. Can we still count on "the testimony of the soul?" Or is that oracle dumb and dead, like the one at Delphi, and at Dodona?

Tertullian, it should be noted, claimed not that some persons have rare and convincing experiences of God, but that *whenever the soul attains its natural soundness, it speaks of God.* It is a fundamental testimony of the soul and not a sporadic one which he asserts. That is equally true in the case of the great mystics of history. They all insist that "the ground of the soul" is divine—"The soul standeth in God," they declare. In its deepest nature it has never "gone out," or separated, from Him. If it did go out and become sundered from God, it would instantly cease to be, as matter would cease to be if it parted from the elemental energy of the universe and went off on its own hook. This is the point which I propose now to consider.

Our sense of obligation, our consciousness of the moral quality of acts, bears witness to a junction of the soul with some spiritual Reality beyond ourselves. I am not maintaining, of course, that we possess within ourselves a private oracle which gives us infallible information on the complicated issues of life. The psalmist said, "I open my mouth and pant for thy commandment," and surely those of us who are not psalmists have prayed, with lips that quivered, for light and help to find our right road at some four-corners where the guide-posts were all down and the night was dark. I am not claiming that we have special information to guide us about the path of duty any more than I should claim that we have it to enlighten us about what medicine to use in disease, or where to bore in the earth's crust for oil. In all these concrete matters and issues of life we must depend upon accumulated experience, and we must find our way by the torch of intelligence which has been put in our hands for just such emergencies, though we certainly can and do accumulate a very sure intuition of what is right for *us*.

But there is something in the very foundation of our self-conscious being that marks the distinction which we call right and wrong. It is as unique and as elemental in us as the distinction of up and down, or of out and in. We may sometimes become confused and mistakenly call up down or down up, but we are never so confused that we do not know that down, whenever we experience it, is always the flat opposite of up. We may fail, too, in a complicated situation to put our finger on the specific act that is *right*, but we always know that right, when it *is* right, cannot be blurred into wrong. This differentiation roots back into the moral ground of the soul. It is a quality of life that could come to light only with the arrival of self-conscious personality. Not to feel the distinction is not to be a fully developed person; not to have the potentiality of that contrast is not yet to have crossed the *divide* between things and persons. The evolution of man from lower non-moral forms of life throws no light on that tremendous reality in us which we call moral obligation. When this conscious feeling of ought "emerged," Adam was born and the sons of God sang for joy over a new creation.

It always seems to the profoundly moral soul that the call of duty, the urge toward goodness, comes from beyond and has its ground in the eternal nature of the universe. Conscience is as truly an organ of relation with a beyond as the physical eye is. The moral quality appears to be at least as objectively real as atoms or solar systems, though of a different order of reality. When we are bringing our personal lives into line with the clearest and highest ethical duty of the hour, we feel ourselves to be revealing here, at a finite point of space and time, a quality of life which is an essential character of the Life of God.

Confucius said, "Our moral being is the great reality (literally the 'great root') of all existence, and the moral order is the universal law of the world."   "All-embracing and vast is the nature of the good man. Profound is he and inexhaustible like a living spring of water, ever running out with life and vitality. All-embracing and vast is he like Heaven. Profound and inexhaustible like the abyss."

"We are begirt," said Emerson, "with laws which execute themselves."   Our moral life, in other words, is part and parcel of the deeper moral life of the universe. When we face a moral issue which may cost us our life and which seems doomed for the moment to temporary defeat, we still go forward and do our deed, knowing well that, *if it is called for*, it will be backed by forces greater than gravitation or electricity. The voice of duty in its highest sweeps carries with it essential confidence in the eternal nature of things. It is one of the noblest testimonies of the soul to the transcending and yet immanent reality of God.

Our conviction of truth is another testimony of the soul. We have no right to use the great word "truth" unless we are ready to grant that there is something within the nature of our personal self that can sweep beyond the particular temporal *fact* which is before the mind and lay hold on some inclusive basis of reality which guarantees the permanent in the midst of the temporal, and which can add *must be* to *is*. Truth is more than something that is now and here. It is something that cannot be otherwise. It is *so* now and always, for me and for all rational minds. It has, at least to our faith, the whole universe behind it.

> It fortifies my soul to know,
> That though I perish, *truth is so*.

The universal and necessary character of truth, without which it is not truth, takes it out of the sphere of things that are contingent and accidental, of things that shift and change, of things that *seem* and *appear*, and gives it an eternal aspect. In so far as we arrive at truth, we are getting in line with something beyond ourselves. We have discovered something that has its ground in a permanent Mind! There may not be many verities in our list which have this exalted standing, but there are some realities which we know cannot be otherwise. They resist all attempts to doubt them. If *they* gave way and collapsed, the universe itself would crumble and cave in and become a "multiverse." All knowledge of every grade would be vitiated and we could say at our leisure what David said in his haste, that "all men are liars," though obviously this remark itself, too, would be a lie!

Whenever the soul in its sanity and rationality bears witness to the truth, it testifies to a deeper Reality with which it is allied, and which binds our fragmentary knowing self to the eternal nature of things. We can *know* only in so far as we are more than we appear to be in our isolation and finiteness. There is a spiritual foundation under our feet. One may as well talk of the music and harmony of a single note as to talk of the *truth* which a single, sundered, finite, insulated mind *knows*. Cut me away from my deep-lying rational roots in the deeper rational Life of God and I can no more talk of truth than an ephemeral gnat in a sunbeam could talk of eternity, or than a sea-urchin could have a theory of space and time.

All of our personal knowledge differentiates into a *subject* that knows an *object*, a self that focuses on a thing that is known. These two aspects of subject and object often seem to us so different and so widely sundered that we are apt to think of them as belonging to two different worlds, one of them mental and the other physical; one as a spiritual reality and the other as a brute, outside fact, mysteriously "presented" to us, by a world of matter. But we cannot hold that crude view a minute if we seriously sound our experience to its depths. Whatever they are, subject and object are not foreign to each other. They are not unrelated. They cannot originate in two different kinds of world. Objects are certainly not "presented" to subjects across unbridged chasms. Subject and object are intelligible only as aspects within one deeper unified consciousness. There is a foundational spiritual reality within us that underspans, or overarches, the differentiation of subject and object. A mind without an object, and an object without a mind that knows it, are each abstractions, and neither one of them exists alone, any more than a "grin" can exist without a face, or a concave side of a curve can exist without a convex side.

The mind, by its very inherent activity, as my friend James Creighton used to say, is already in touch with a reality which is of kindred nature to itself. Subject and object are always united in the total context of experience, and the "context of experience" is a rich concrete, never a dry, abstract affair. It has both an inside and an outside aspect held together in living unity. If you once begin your theory of knowledge by assuming an inside mind that is spiritual and an outside fact that is physical, no amount of wooing, as I have already said, will ever bring that estranged couple to a happy marriage. The world we actually experience is never a world of bare physical facts; it is always a world crammed with human interests, with so-called subjective aspects as well as objective aspects, touched with beauty and sublimity, awakening us to aims and pursuits of truth, challenging us with mysteries to be solved, calling us to moral tasks, and showing itself to us as the polar complement to our inner life. If knowledge is to be in any real sense *knowledge*, it must carry with it the implications of a universe that is in essence spiritual, and our own spirit that does the knowing must be rounded by a greater Spirit,

Whose dwelling is the light of setting suns.

It is a hopeless task to try to conjure up something spiritual if you begin with an undivine world of sheer mechanism, utterly devoid of Spirit. The testimony of the soul is an absurd claim, if, after all, the soul is only an alien and foreign spiritual habitant moving about in a world of dead, clanking matter.

Our entire business of living for ideal ends lifts us out of the level of "things" and proclaims us to belong to a spiritual order. We rise above what the world reports as *fact*. We travel on ahead of all roads that have been built. We see what *might be*, even while as yet it is not. As Professor Whitehead puts it, "Our minds build cathedrals before the workmen have moved a stone, and our minds destroy them before the elements have worn down their arches." By the bending of the light rays, we can see the sun in the morning before it rises. So too, in this higher sphere of life, we can discover what ought to be before it is built. The Kingdom of God is a

vision in a soul before it is an accomplished fact
of history.   Everything supremely great in this
world has lived as a dream in somebody's soul
before it has had a local habitation and a name.

This seems to me to be one of the most significant spiritual testimonies the soul ever utters.
Sometimes we blunder here with our ideals as we
also blunder in our affirmation of duty and truth.
We sometimes mistake a mirage for real water.
We build our city of God on cloud wracks instead
of four-square here among men, but the point is
this: we are inherently ideal-builders.   We transcend the patterns which our senses show us.   We
are not content to copy what is given.   We carry
a higher model in our bosoms.   We see beyond
the *is*.   We think beyond what is presented to us.
We leap ahead of what is finished.   Descartes
was struggling with something very real when he
said that we should not be so conscious of finiteness if we did not have the idea of infinity all the
time within our consciousness.   Kant, too, always
found himself confronted with a higher Reason
in himself which pushed out beyond the confines
of what could be tabulated and described and
pigeon-holed.   We take account of only part of
ourselves, we reduce our heritage as men, when
we make what *is*, or what *has been*, the measure

of our sphere. "We grant that human life is mean," wrote Emerson, "but how did we find out that it is mean? What is the ground of this uneasiness; of this old discontent? What is the universal sense of want and ignorance, but the fine innuendo by which the soul makes its enormous claim?" And in his *Journal* he wrote these moving words: "The best part of truth is certainly that which hovers in gleams and suggestions, unpossessed, before man. His recorded knowledge is dead and cold. But this chorus of thoughts and hopes, these dawning truths, like great stars just lifting themselves into his horizon, they are his future and console him for the ridiculous brevity and meanness of his civic life."

"What's strange," Dostoevsky wrote in *The Brothers Karamazov*, "what would be marvelous, is not that God should really exist; the marvel is that such an idea, the idea of the necessity of God, could enter the head of such a savage, vicious beast as man. So holy it is, so touching, so wise and so great credit it does to man."

We never stop at the margin, the frontier, of the visible and tangible. It is impossible to stop there. Our world floods over all such frontiers and we always live out beyond the perilous edges of space and time, of what has been and is, of what we see and touch, of what we know and describe. We could not get on for a minute with a bounded, finite world which had definite, unjumpable limits and abrupt terminal fences. We seldom realize how much we draw upon this beyond, how we eke out the scanty fare of the here and now by generous drafts from the other side of the frontiers. This tendency to live beyond what is given in sense experience and to transcend all our boundaries is due to something spiritual in the very nature of our being. It is not by accident that we are ideal-forming persons. It is not so much "in our blood" as it is in the structure of our interior self, whatever that may turn out to be. There is a "more yet" linked up with every experience, whether it comes from without or from within. There is a peripheral halo around every focus-point on which we fix eye or mind. We look down upon our deeds from above and judge them in the light of a larger ideal. We approve or disapprove of our present self by reference to something more. We look before and after, and see "the being that we are" always in a luminous perspective, never as a finished "thing."

We have our experiences of *value*, of beauty, of truth, and of goodness, just because we are not single-level, one-track beings. We are quite willing to be told that we are curiously carved pieces of the earth's crust, or strange dust-wreath vortexes, if we may add to the account *the something more which we know we are*. The whirling dust-wreaths of the street do not have longings. The bits of earth crust which we throw about with our shovel do not yearn for what is not and then forthwith construct it. Desires and strivings, visions and ideals, emotions and sentiments, are as much a genuine part of us as are the iron and lime and phosphorus in our bodies. We have insights of what ought to be, appreciations of beauty, convictions of truth, experiences of love, and these things are not part of the earth's crust. They are not physical realities. They are not *results* of masses of matter in motion. They cannot be adequately explained mechanically. They are real for mind and only for mind. But they are not purely *subjective*. They refer to some reality beyond the individual. They are not arbitrary. They are not capricious. They are not visionary. It is by them that we truly live. They are revealed through us rather than created by us. They *find* us. They awaken us. They break in upon us from beyond us. They call us forth to be organs of their revealing. They enrich us.

They expand us. They help us to realize our lives as nothing else does. They point to a world of a higher type than that of matter, a world closely linked with our minds but at the same time overarching and vaster. That higher, overbrimming world which is the source of these values must be a world of Spirit, for truth and beauty and goodness have significance only for an appreciative spirit. When the soul loves and enjoys these things, it thereby bears its testimony to a spiritual reality as the ground of ideal values, as the source of these intrinsic qualities.

Little Joe in *Bleak House* was trying to get his uneasy sleep in a London alley when a policeman turned his bull's-eye light on him and said, "Move on out of this. You can't sleep here." With pitiful tone the little fellow said, "I've been moving on ever since I was born." "I can't help that," was the gruff answer, "move on again." "But where to?" came the deep question from the child. It is not a policeman that awakens *us* and tells us to move on out of our alleys and camping places. It is a gentle and a friendly inner voice that sends us forward. Sometimes it comes as a trumpet-call that challenges us to move on:

> Ever and anon a trumpet sounds
> From the hid battlements of eternity.

No doubt I shall be answered that there are innumerable persons who hear no trumpets out of time or eternity, and who are not aware of any urge to "move on." They eat and drink, sleep and wake, work and get, and they are satisfied with the now and here. If the facts are thus as affirmed, one would be compelled to admit that there is a type of person who carries no beyond within himself, and whose life is bounded by the needs of his circulation and digestion, the waste and repair of his body cells. I must first be convinced that there are such men. They are as unknown to me as are the Pigmies or the one-eyed Arimaspians. If there are self-conscious beings who do not transcend themselves, who are not haunted by eternity, who live in what is already won, and have no dreams of what is unwon, they do not belong to my species. They range under a different class-order. I only know that my kind of men have

> Hints of occasion infinite
> To keep the soul alert with noble discontent
> And onward yearnings of unstilled desire.

It is this capacity in us for overpassing what *is* and of living forward into what ought to be that makes us essentially religious beings. We are endowed with vision for more inclusive wholes than any our eyes have seen, and so long as we preserve our fundamental nature as men we shall be religious, we shall keep on our quest for God, and we shall enjoy our glimpses of Him. Professor Whitehead has already said what I want to say at this point. "Religion," he says, "is the vision of something that stands beyond, behind and within the passing flux of immediate things; something which is real and yet waiting to be realized; something which is a remote posibility, and yet the greatest of present facts; something which gives meaning to all that passes, and yet eludes apprehension; something whose possession is the final good, and yet is beyond all reach; something which is the ultimate ideal and the hopeless quest.[1]

But besides all this, there is another testimony of the soul which from ancient times has been called the mystical experience. There apparently always have been persons in the world, and there still are such persons, who bear witness to a consciousness of an environing and invading larger life, surrounding their own tiny "bank and shoal" of being.

Confucius, whom we usually regard as unmystical, wrote: "The power of spiritual forces in

[1] *Science and the Modern World*, p. 275.

the Universe—how active it is everywhere! Invisible to the eyes and impalpable to the senses, it is inherent in all things, and nothing can escape its operation. . . . Like the rush of mighty waters, the presence of unseen Powers is felt, sometimes above us, sometimes around us."

"God is nearer to us than our soul," Lady Julian of Norwich declared. "He is the ground in whom our soul standeth."

"I am as sure as that I live that nothing is so near to me as God," is Eckhart's testimony.

"United without intermediary to the Spirit of God, we can meet God and possess with Him and in Him our eternal blessedness," wrote the Flemish mystic Jan Ruysbroeck.

Beethoven said to a friend one day, "I well know that God is nearer to me than others are. I commune with Him."

Henri Bergson has said, in our time, that genuine philosophy is "the turning of the mind homeward, the coincidence of human consciousness with the living principle from which it emanates, a contact with the creative effort."

Josiah Royce, toward the end of his life, said: "Unless, in moments of peace, of illumination, of hope, of devotion, of inward vision, you have seemed to feel the presence of your Deliverer, unless it has sometimes *seemed* to you as if the way to the homeland of the spirit were opened to your sight by a revelation as from the divine, unless this privilege has been yours, the way to a higher growth in insight will be slow and uncertain to you."

Metchnikoff, the life-long scientist, went to his death saying as his last words: "Do not fear for me; I have had a Divine light."

My dear friend, the late Baron Friedrich von Hügel, wrote to a friend in America in 1922 about the two levels of life and thought, the scientific and the religious levels, both of which he felt were necessary for a complete life. "For myself," he said, "I must have both movements: the palace of my soul must have somehow two lifts—a lift which is always going up from below (the scientific movement) and a lift which is always going down from above (the religious movement). I must be seeking and be having. I must both move and repose."

This array of testimony comes from many lands and from many generations. It comes from ignorant persons and learned, from saints and from those who would prefer to be called secular persons. It could be multiplied a thousand-fold. Those who have written about their experience of God in any case form only a tiny fraction of those who have *had* the experience and who have lived in the power of it.

This mystical capacity in us, this capacity for another kind of world than that in space and composed of matter, *underlies*, as I have said, both our highest moral and religious attainments. It is *that* which has made us moral and religious beings, and it would in some measure survive any disaster which might sweep away all our codified laws and existent institutions, even all our sacred books and creeds and churches.

The moment we realize clearly that God is not in the sky, but *is Spirit*, and therefore is the Over-Spirit of our own finite spirits, all our religious problems are at once affected by the discovery. We no longer are interested in the immense structure which human thought and imagination have builded to glorify the imperial sovereign of the sky, with His court of angelic and seraphic beings and with His gorgeous pictorial heaven above the dome of the sky. Our religion ceases to be other-worldly in the ancient sense, and is primarily concerned with the opening out of our own inner selves to the divine influences of the Spirit that environs our central being. God is to be found and known, not in terms of astronomy, but rather

in terms of our noblest ethical and spiritual aspirations. He is best revealed by what is best
in man. In his deepest nature man is spirit, and
so is in very truth made in the image of God and
on the way toward Him. Finite and fragmentary
we certainly are, "broken lights" of the one light,
as Tennyson puts it, but in any case God and
man are not sundered in the sense that mind and
matter have been held to be separated by an impassable "divide." The divine and the human are
not two diverse and incompatible realities, one
exclusive of the other. No one can be a *person*
in the full meaning of the word and not partake
of God, the complete Spirit, any more than a
river can be a river without partaking of the
ocean, or than an atom can be an atom without
partaking of electrical energy. The traits that
are essential to personality are exhibited in fullness only in that complete Spirit whom we name
God and who alone can say, *I am*; but even in our
finite and fragmentary state we are all the time
reaching beyond our own narrow limits and drawing upon the larger spiritual Life that overspans
us, as the tiny arc of a circle points to and implies
the whole curve. God in fact is all that we are
striving to be. To find Him we do not need to
travel off into space or backward in time, but

rather to go down to profounder levels of spiritual life. The Person in all human history who found Him most truly and revealed Him best did so by opening out all the potential levels of His deepest nature to the Spirit of God, so that the human and the divine were for once harmoniously united in one life.

The process of reaching new levels and profounder deeps of being is both an outward and an inward process. The lessons of history, the testimony of the ethical experience of the race, the illumination of Christ's revelation, are priceless agencies of enlargement and inspiration. But none of these, nor all of them, can take the place of those inner processes by which one reaches new interior levels of being and liberates in the inmost depth of the soul currents of influence which connect directly with the environing Life of God.

William James called this larger Life "a More of Consciousness continuous and conterminous with our own." Whittier, who was himself a potent witness of this mystical experience, declared:

> So sometimes comes to soul and sense
> The feeling which is evidence,
> That near about us lies
> The realm of spiritual mysteries.

The sphere of the supernal powers
Impinges on this world of ours.

The testimony to such realities has usually been so presented that it gives the impression that these experiences are rare and unusual occurrences, limited to unique individuals and consequently throwing little light on the fundamental nature of the human soul as such. I am convinced that this impression needs revision. All of the great capacities of the soul come to light best, of course, in persons who are geniuses. The whole range and scope of music have been enlarged since we have heard what Bach could do with it, and we know how painting can express the inner depth of a face because Raphael has exhibited unexpected possibilities in his Sistine Madonna. So, too, the reality of God and the nearness of His Life to the soul of man reach a height of assurance in the experience of St. Paul, St. Francis, Jacob Boehme, and George Fox that they do not usually reach with more ordinary persons. But I am convinced that a great many of these so-called "ordinary" persons have a sense of contact with spiritual forces that give their lives an extraordinary effectiveness.

Every time I visit a new place anywhere in America or abroad and stay long enough to become well acquainted with conditions, I always discover some person in the region who is a hundred-horsepower person and whose life is raising the whole moral and spiritual level of the community.

These dynamic persons whom I am endeavoring to describe are, of course, always unconscious of possessing unusual grace or power. They go about their tasks of love and service with a certain ease and naturalness that attend all work done by "second nature." One fine feature, too, of their contribution is that it usually comes as a by-product of their lives—not as the main thing aimed at. Generally they are very busy persons, overloaded with their own life-work, but that in no way prevents them from being transmitters, because they are steadied and stabilized with a weighty occupation. The peculiar thing is that they are always *there* when something needs to be done for the church or for the community, or for a sick neighbor or for some central cause that would fall without a strong hand and a consecrated spirit behind it. The kind of person I keep discovering in my travels works on without fuss, worry or friction, without jealousy or ambition, and is concerned only to help to make things go forward.

As you watch these practical saints operate, in a great variety of affairs and under very different conditions, you soon see that their supreme asset is personality; though, of course, they do not in the least suspect it, nor do those who follow their leadership know very clearly why they follow so naturally.   They possess a certain swift, and more or less sure, sense of direction and a kind of intuition as to what ought to be done.   It is natural for them to plan and decide, natural also for them to feel confident and to inspire confidence in others.   I have no doubt that in many instances such persons are born with peculiar gifts and endowments.   But those whom I have known best have had something more than natural equipments.   They have been "transmitters," as I have said, of forces whose source was beyond themselves.   When love, joy, peace, good temper, kindliness, generosity, fidelity, gentleness, and self-control appear in a life—appear continuously and in a triumphant quality—we may as well conclude with St. Paul that these traits are the fruit and harvest of the Spirit.   They furnish the best evidences there are that the life which reveals them has come into contact with God.

St. Paul prayed that his friends might have "peace and joy in believing."   He evidently thought that a faith which had the demonstration of peace and joy was more to be desired than one that conformed with some external standard. In fact, interior traits of spiritual life and power outweigh all other tests of fellowship with Christ. These persons whom I find so effective in their communities are sometimes very zealous in their conformity to ancient standards; and, again, sometimes they think nothing whatever about external standards. In these matters it is largely a question of their education and the religious climate in which they have lived. In any case, the effective factor is never the quality of conformity or of non-conformity, but the formation of a rich, Christlike spirit which makes them radiant and dynamic.

This way of life is the noblest form of mysticism. It is the practice, often the unconscious practice, of the presence of God. I have often felt, as I have watched these rural saints, these makers of community spirit, these builders of the kingdom of love and peace, a kind of majestic sense of awe. They seem to be lending their hands to a larger Life than their own. If they were asked, they would deny that they were mystics. "No, I am not a mystic. I have no mighty experiences. I am too practical and too commonplace ever to be a mystic." My answer would be that there is no inconsistency between a mystical life and a practical life. The more truly mystical a person is, the greater the probability that he will be effectively practical. God reveals Himself in many ways, and any way that lets His Life break through and form the atmosphere and spirit of a village, of a church, of a school, a college, a Sunday School, or a home is a revelation of God, and the person, who is in some sense the fresh, present-day organ of the Life of God, is just so far a practical mystic.

Many years ago Elizabeth Stuart Phelps wrote a widely read story called *A Singular Life*. Its hero was one of these high-powered saints of whom I have been telling. He changed many lives from low-power efficiency to high-power efficiency. He reduced the forces of evil and widened the area of light. He quickened pure unselfish love and he exhibited a noble type of sacrificial spirit. He was what I mean by a practical mystic.

I am contending that such lives as these are not "singular" lives. The high-power life is the normal life, and such lives are more numerous than the "Who's Who among Saints" would lead us to expect. I meet them on trains, on ocean steamers, on holiday trips, and on casual walks, and, as I have said, wherever I stay long enough to get acquainted with any neighborhood that I visit. They are the outstanding evidences of Christianity. They are worth a thousand editions of Paley's *Evidences*. They walk about their ordinary tasks of life without knowing that their faces shine, but they are in the true apostolic succession, and they live in the demonstration of the Spirit and power. Evelyn Underhill agrees with this position which I have been interpreting, and she has very clearly expressed it in her excellent book, *The Mystics of the Church*. She says:

> We cannot say that there is a separate "mystical sense," which some men have and some have not, but rather that every human soul has a certain latent capacity for God, and that in some this capacity is realized with an astonishing richness. Such a realization may be of many kinds and degrees—personal or impersonal, abrupt and ecstatic, or peaceful and continuous. This will depend partly on the temperament of the mystic, and partly on his religious background and education.

If we take all these experiences together—appearing as they do wherever religion becomes a living interest to men—we find that they are, as